HIGH FLYER

UPPER INTERMEDIATE

Students' Book

ANA ACEVEDO
MARISOL GOWER
Consultant for Romanian Materials: Adriana Tepelea

LONGMAN

Contents

Contents

Contents

Additional material page 102   Grammar reference page 107

Contents

Journeys past and present

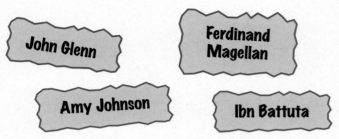

John Glenn

Ferdinand Magellan

Amy Johnson

Ibn Battuta

I Find out about these important travellers.

a) Match them with the notes which follow.

1 Born in Portugal in 1480, he was the first man to find a sea route from the Atlantic Ocean to the Pacific, round the tip of the American continent.

2 Born in 1921, he was the first American to orbit the Earth in 1962. Returned to space, aged 77, to conduct experiments on the process of ageing.

3 Born in Morocco in 1304, he travelled to Persia (Iran), Asia Minor (Turkey) and Northern India and across the Sahara to Timbuktu. His descriptions tell us a lot about the Muslim world in the Middle Ages.

4 Born in 1903 in Hull, England, this pilot was the first woman to fly to Australia. She flew to Japan, to Cape Town and America. Her aircraft fell into the sea in 1941 in mysterious circumstances.

b) Suggest the means of transport the travellers probably used to get to their destinations.

HIGH FLYERS

A LONG TIME AGO, a young man, called Icarus, wanted to fly like a bird. He made himself a pair of wings, using wax. He flew so high that he got too
5 near the sun. The heat melted his wings and he fell to earth and died. So goes the story in classical Greek mythology.

Man has always wanted to fly.
10 Many people have devoted their lives to building flying machines. Many have died in the process. We have been travelling by air for such a long time that it is easy to forget the
15 achievements of the pioneers which have made it possible for us to fly.

The first person to fly did so in 1783 with a hot-air balloon designed by the Montgolfier brothers in
20 France. The first hydrogen-filled balloons flew in the same year. These balloons carried passengers until the 1930s. People have continued to fly balloons since then, but mostly for
25 pleasure or sport.

The next development after balloons was the airship, or dirigible. This was a sausage-shaped balloon powered by an engine. The
30 first flight of an airship, *La France*, was in 1884. Many huge hydrogen-filled airships were built to carry large numbers of passengers. On 6 May 1937 the world's longest
35 airship, the *Hindenburg*, burst into flames just before it moored in New York, killing 35 of the 97 people on board. Airships have not been used again since that accident.
40 There have been many other exciting developments in the last hundred years. In the USA, Orville and Wilbur Wright built *The Flyer*, a biplane (with two sets of wings)
45 where the pilot lay flat across the lower wing. Bicycle chains and gears connected the engine to two propellers which turned at about 450 times per minute. On 17 December
50 1903, Orville Wright made a 12 second flight over a distance of 36 metres. This was the first aeroplane flight in history. In 1909, Louis Blériot flew across the English
55 Channel. Ten years later, Alcock and Brown made the first non-stop flight across the Atlantic.

Passenger flying developed after World War 1. During the 1920s,
60 passengers flew aboard mail planes, but by the late 1930s, flying was much more luxurious. Jets were mainly developed after World War 2. The first jet airliner entered service in
65 1952. The Boeing 747 'jumbo jet' was the first of the wide-bodied jets. Jet plane manufacturers have been improving their machines constantly; the latest versions can carry over 600
70 passengers and fly a third of the way round the world non-stop. Today, nearly all long-distance international travel is by jet.

The wealthy can travel on
75 Concorde, the first supersonic airliner. Concorde has been carrying people around the world since its launch in 1969. It can carry up to 144 passengers at twice the speed of
80 sound and can cross the Atlantic in three hours.

Now that air travel is a common experience, man has turned his attention to the conquest of space. It
85 isn't yet possible for you or me to travel into space for a holiday but you can be sure that someone, somewhere, is working to make this possible, perhaps during our lifetime.

Reading

Skimming means reading a text quickly to get an idea of the organisation and the main ideas in the text. Read the beginnings and the ends of paragraphs; that is where the main ideas are. Skimming a text will make a detailed reading easier.

2 **Look at the article on the page opposite. Read the title and look at the pictures. Then skim the text. Circle the description that fits the article best.**

1   This is an article about the Wright brothers and their flying machine. The main point of the text is the contribution they made to flying.
2   The article is about the history of flying. It describes the different ways of flying man has invented.
3   This text is about the first man who managed to fly, the equipment he used and how he died.

3 **Reread the article. Write the dates of each event. Number the events 1–6, in chronological order.**

__ the first flight of an airship
__ the first non-stop flight across the Atlantic
__ the first aeroplane flight in history
__ the first flight of a jet airliner
__ the last journey of an airship
__ the first crossing of the English Channel by plane

Grammar

Present Perfect

1   Many people **have devoted** their lives to building flying machines.
It's a past event but we don't mention exactly when it happened: it happened at an unspecified time in the past and it may happen again.

2   The achievements of the pioneers **have made** it possible for us to fly.
The present situation, that we are able to fly, is the result of the past work of the pioneers.

3   Man **has** always **wanted** to fly.
Man's desire to fly began in the past and still exists.

Present Perfect Continuous

4   People **have been travelling** by jet since the early 1950s.
We are emphasising the duration of the action which started in the past and is still happening.

4 **Put the verbs in brackets in either the *Present Perfect* or the *Present Perfect Continuous*.**

1   Richard Branson, owner of Virgin Atlantic, _____ (fly) balloons for many years. He still flies them today.
2   I know he _____ (make) a transatlantic flight, but I'm not sure when.
3   _____ you ever _____ (see) a hot-air balloon?
4   Scientists _____ (work) on a new plane but the work is not finished yet.
5   John Glenn _____ (orbit) the Earth many times in his life.
6   Mir, the space station, _____ (orbit) the Earth non-stop since 1986.
7   Captain Lewis is a very experienced Concorde pilot. He _____ (fly) the supersonic plane for ten years.
8   They _____ (build) a new terminal in the city so more airlines can use the airport now.

5 **Some of the time expressions below can only be used to complete sentence 2 correctly; some to complete 1 and 2; one expression cannot be used with either. Write out the completed sentences.**

since six o'clock	all day	already
two months ago	recently	often
for a long time	before	once

1 She has been driving ...   **2** He has driven ...

6 **Write true sentences about yourself using the clues in brackets ( ), as in the example. Be careful: you need to add *for* or *since*.**

1   I/play (your favourite sport)/(the duration).
    I have been playing football for three years.
2   My family and I/live in (your town)/(the date).
3   I/study at (the name of your school)/(number of years).
4   My father/work at (his place of work)/(starting date).
5   I/learn English/(school year).
6   (Your best friend) and I/be best friends/(year when you met).

7 How do people in your class travel?

a) Ask and answer these questions in your class.

1 How do you travel to school?
2 How long does your journey take?
3 How much do you spend on transport a week?
4 Why did you choose your means of transport?
5 How long have you been using this means of transport?
6 Have you tried any other means of transport? Which?

b) Make a chart of your results. Then answer these questions.

1 What is the most popular form of transport?
2 How long do people travel, on average, per day?
3 How much do people spend on transport, on average, per week?
4 Has anyone tried any other ways of travelling to school? Which?

8 Read this student's composition. How many means of transport does he mention? How many of them exist in your town?

Journeys past and present in London

By Mickey Owen

In 1800 London was home to about one million people, fewer than today's rush hour travellers! By 1900, London was the biggest city in the world, with a population of over six million. As the city grew, new kinds of transport were needed. This
5 project is about the history of bus services in London.
The first London omnibus service was introduced by George Shillibeer in 1829. The omnibuses were pulled by horses. By 1834 there were 376 licensed omnibuses in London. In 1858, the London General Omnibus Company took over three-
10 quarters of the smaller companies. In 1870 the first horse tram began running. It ran along tracks which lay level with the road surface. They were cheap and could carry as many passengers as the horse buses. The public was impressed and the trams were an instant success. However, horses were
15 expensive to keep and feed, so transport companies looked for alternative means of power. Trams became powered by electricity from overhead wires and buses by diesel engines.
London Transport, the state-owned company formed in 1933, gradually got rid of trams. London's red buses, especially
20 the *Routemaster,* introduced in 1956, have been a symbol of London since then. In 1985 the government encouraged other bus companies to offer services within the capital. Since September 1994 all London buses have been run by privately-owned companies.
25 My family has lived in London for several generations and my grandfather worked as a bus conductor for thirty years. He has seen many changes in the transport system. I have been using buses all my life and, in my opinion, riding on the top of a double-decker is not only convenient but also the best way to
30 enjoy the sights of our city.

9 Answer these questions about Mickey's composition.

1 Why do you think Mickey chose this topic?
2 What do you think the traffic was like in London in the late 19th century?
3 Why do you think the transport companies decided to stop using horses?
4 Why do you think red buses became so famous around the world?
5 Why do you think private companies were encouraged to offer transport services?

Grammar

Collective nouns

1 The public **was** impressed by the new trams.
(*We think of the public as a single unit.*)

2 The public **were** impressed by the new trams.
(*We think of the public as a number of individuals.*)

Look!

You can use a plural verb after a collective noun, but collective nouns cannot be pluralised.

✗ Some ~~publics~~ ~~liked omnibuses.~~
✔ Some **members of the public** liked omnibuses.

Many collective nouns have other meanings in which they are countable.
The **team** have been wearing the same colours for years.
(*It's a particular team.*)
Some **teams** have worn the same colours for years.
(*They are several different teams.*)

Listening

12 🔊 **A group is visiting the London Transport Museum.**

a) Listen and mark these statements T (true) or F (false).

1 The guide is explaining the history of London Transport.
2 The group is interested in the information.
3 The group understood all the guide's explanations.

b) Listen again. Tick the points the group didn't understand at first.

1 what is special about the Metropolitan line	4 when Queen Victoria lived
2 the working hours of underground staff	5 the job 'fluffers' do
3 the method of changing a rail	6 the meaning of 'fluff'

c) Listen again. List the phrases used to ask for clarification of the points in **b)**, and those which give clarification.

Asking for clarification

Do you mean the first underground railway ever, or just in London?

Clarifying your message

I mean the world's first …

Get talking

13 **Prepare to describe and draw a picture.**

STUDENT A: Look at page xix. Follow the instructions there.
STUDENT B: Look at page xx. Follow the instructions there.

Writing

★ *The process of writing consists of different stages, from planning to editing your work. If you follow the steps and rewrite bits you are not happy with, your writing in English will improve.*

14 **Prepare to write a composition.**

a) You are going to write about transport in your home area. Number the steps below in the order in which you would do them.

__ check my grammar, spelling and punctuation
2 write down lots of ideas
3 make a plan, including an introduction and a conclusion
4 write a first draft of my composition
5 select and order the ideas I want to use and make notes
__ check that each paragraph has a main idea (in a topic sentence) and good supporting details

b) The title of your composition is *'Journeys past and present in (your town)'*. Use the information you gathered in exercise 7. Follow the steps you have numbered in **a)**. Mickey's composition will give you ideas on how to organise your composition.

10 **Each of the following sentences has one mistake. Underline the mistake and correct it.**

1 The family have always been close and it gets together every Sunday.
2 The company are very proud of the new bus service it has launched.
3 The staffs on the Underground have got new uniforms.
4 All the medias have reported the accident.
5 England have lost all its games so far.

11 **Write sentences about the topics below.**

EXAMPLE: *My community is small. It has only got 1,200 inhabitants.*

your community
your favourite football team
the media in your country
your family
the staff in your favourite shop
the behaviour of the public at sports events

The world's a stage

1 In pairs, ask and answer.

1 Have you ever been to the theatre? If so, what have you seen?
2 What do you think is the difference between theatre and cinema?

Reading

⭐ *Remember that when you need to find specific information in a text, you don't have to read all of it. **Scan** the text (look through it to find the relevant parts, with the information you need).*

2 Scan the leaflet. Complete the sentences.

1 The name of the play is _____ .
2 _____ is the director.
3 The play is on at the _____ in Birmingham.
4 The cheapest matinée ticket is £_____.
5 If you go on a school trip, you only pay £_____ for some performances.

3 Now read the information inside the leaflet. Answer the questions.

1 How did the German critics react to *Oresteia*?
2 Do British audiences know Purcarete's work?
3 What was his adaptation of *Phaedra* like?
4 When was *Les Danaïdes* performed in Dublin?
5 When did British audiences see his *Titus Andronicus*?

offshore
international cultural projects present

ORESTEIA

A VERSION OF THE TRILOGY FOR ONE EVENING

ADAPTED AND DIRECTED BY SILVIU PURCARETE

NATIONAL THEATRE OF CRAIOVA, ROMANIA

TICKET PRICES
EVENINGS ---Tue – Fri   £7.25, £10.50, £13.50, £15.50, £17.50
---------------Sat   £8.75, £12.50, £15.50, £17.50, £19.00

MATINÉE -----(1.30pm) £7.25, £8.00, £10.00, £11.50, £12.50

DISCOUNTS
CONCESSIONS: Over 60s, children, registered disabled, recipients of jobseeker's allowance, family credit, income support and students – £2 off (excluding previews)

SCHOOL/STUDENT GROUPS: £6.50 (Selected perfs only). One ticket free with every 15 students.

GROUPS: 6–9 SAVE 10%, 10–39 SAVE 15%, 40+ SAVE 20% (Mon-Fri only)

STAND-BY: Students, registered disabled, recipients of jobseekers' allowance – £5 (from 1pm on day of performance)

(ONLY ONE SAVING APPLIES PER TICKET AND ALL TICKETS AND SAVINGS ARE SUBJECT TO AVAILABILITY)

20–24 October @ 7.30pm (Sat mat 1.30pm)
Birmingham Rep, Centenary Square, Broad Street, Birmingham B1 2EP
Tickets £7.25 - £19.00

Birmingham
REP   BOX OFFICE 0121 236 4455

BOX OFFICE 0121 236 4455

Grammar

> **Position of adverbials**
>
> **1 Where? Adverbials of place**
> *Usually at the end:* Purcarete's haunting theatrical style is well known **in the UK and Ireland.**
>
> **2 When? Adverbials of time**
> *At the beginning:* **The following year**, audiences in Dublin were enthralled by 'Les Danaïdes'.
> *At the end:* His controversial 'Titus Andronicus' amazed audiences **in 1997.**
> The new or important information usually goes at the end of the sentence.
>
> **3 How? Adverbials of manner**
> *Usually after the verb phrase:* Aeschylus' drama explores the conflict between duty and morality **passionately.**
> *Before the main verb if there is an auxiliary:* 'Phaedra' was **beautifully** adapted in 1995.
>
> **4 What order?**
> *Usually how + where + when:* The critics praised Pucarete's adaptation **highly in the German press in the summer.**

The renowned theatre director Silviu Purcarete brings *Oresteia* – his newest adaptation of an Aeschylus tragedy – to four of the largest stages in Britain and Ireland this autumn.

Premiered at the Recklinghausen Festival, this epic brought audiences to their feet. The critics praised Pucarete's adaptation highly in the German press in the summer.

Purcarete's haunting theatrical style is well known in the UK and Ireland. *Phaedra* was beautifully adapted in 1995.

The following year, audiences in Birmingham, Glasgow and Dublin were enthralled by *Les Danaïdes*. His controversial *Titus Andronicus* amazed audiences in 1997. *Oresteia* continues Purcarete's fascination with ancient classical texts and their timeless themes. 'My taste is for classical literature because it's the most modern literature possible,' he explains. Aeschylus' drama of family murder and revenge explores the conflict between duty and morality passionately.

Pucarete's special gifts as a visual director make the most of the story. 'I try to create an image that should be clear for a modern audience,' the director explains.

Performed in Romanian with English surtitles.

RESTEIA

4 Unscramble the sentences to find out the plot of *Oresteia*. Careful! There may be more than one possibility for some sentences.

EXAMPLE: *Before the trilogy begins, King Agamemnon sacrifices his daughter to save his fleet.*

1 King Agamemnon/before the trilogy begins/to save his fleet/sacrifices his daughter

2 the King/after the Trojan war/to Argos/returns

3 looking for revenge/Queen Clytemnestra/bitterly/is

4 and her lover Aegisthus/she/at the end of the first play/kill Agamemnon

5 waits/for her brother Orestes to return/anxiously/Agamemnon's daughter Electra

6 to revenge her father's death/she/wants him/immediately

7 Clytemnestra and Aegisthus/just inside the palace doors/kills/Orestes

8 at the Acropolis in Athens/is/tried/Orestes/formally

9 thoughtfully/casts her vote/Athena, goddess of wisdom,

10 Orestes/from the ancient blood vengeance/quickly/is/released

5 Have you got acting talent? Get into groups of 4–5.

a) Choose one of the adverbs of manner below. Write it down but don't let anybody see it.

b) Take turns to mime actions your group asks you to in the manner of the adverb you have chosen.

c) Can the rest of the group guess the adverb?

EXAMPLE:

EMIL: *Comb your hair in the manner of the adverb, Adriana.*

VLAD: *You're combing your hair delicately.*

ADRIANA: *No, not delicately.*

ALEXANDRA: *Have a cup of coffee in the manner of the adverb.*

CATALINA: *I know! You're drinking a cup of coffee gracefully.*

ADRIANA: *Yes, I am.*

carelessly	delicately	dramatically
fiercely	gracefully	hurriedly
tenderly	thoughtfully	·vigorously

Get talking

6 🔊 Listen to the three dialogues. Which play:

1 has been on for more than 50 years?
2 is going to be performed in a month's time?
3 has a secret ending?
4 is hilarious?
5 is a text studied at school?
6 is an example of the 'theatre of the absurd'?

7 Listen again. Write down the phrases used to:

1 invite someone (3 phrases).
2 accept an invitation.
3 refuse an invitation.
4 express uncertainty.

Add at least one more phrase to 1–4 above. Mark the expressions F (formal) or I (informal).

8 Where would you like to go? Who will you invite?

a) Make a list of three events you would like to go to.

b) In pairs, take turns to invite and respond to your partner's invitations to these events.

The person inviting chooses a formal or an informal way. The person responding has to use a similar level of formality.

Listening

 Listening to conversations seems less difficult if you remember that people:

- *talk in short sentences which are not always grammatically complete.*
- *repeat things, interrupt one another or pause in mid-sentence.*
- *sometimes start saying something, then change their minds and say something different.*
- *sometimes change the topic suddenly.*
- *use 'fillers' ('well', 'er'), attention getters ('look'), expressions of surprise ('oh no').*
- *use different intonation patterns to convey meaning.*

9 **Listen to Jamie, his Aunt Kitty and Uncle Tony talking after they saw** *Oresteia.* **Put your hand up as you hear:**

- a pause
- a repetition
- a filler
- a sudden change of topic
- a false start
- an attention getter

10 **Three of the basic intonation patterns in English are:**

Fall ⤸   Rise ⤷   Level ⇒

Listen to these sentences from the dialogue and mark them F ⤸, R ⤷ or L ⇒ .

1 Did you like it, Jamie?
2 Purcarete's done it in a very modern way, almost like a film.
3 How much have you studied the classics?
4 Another boring book I have to read.
5 But then the teacher started to explain.

11 **Listen to the complete dialogue again. Mark the sentences T (true) or F (false). Correct the false sentences.**

1 Jamie enjoyed watching the scenes he'd read.
2 Aunt Kitty likes looking at the masks.
3 Uncle Tony prefers having women play female roles.
4 Jamie would like to see men playing women's roles.
5 When he started reading the book he thought it would be boring.
6 When his teacher began to explain he understood it better.
7 Aunt Kitty didn't mind not understanding the Romanian.
8 She didn't mind having to read the surtitles.

Grammar

Verbs followed by gerund

1 *Verb* { (+ not) + *verb* –ing
(somebody)

I enjoyed watching the scenes I'd read.
I didn't mind not understanding the Romanian.
I'd **imagined the actors wearing** masks.
Other verbs: appreciate, avoid, consider, contemplate, delay, deny, detest, dislike, enjoy, excuse, forgive, can't help, imagine, mention, (don't) mind, miss, postpone, practise, resent, resist, risk, can't stand

1 *Verb* (+ not) + *verb* –ing
                              or
                              verb infinitive
It is more common to use the infinitive when referring to one particular occasion.
I like looking at the faces.
I'd **like to see** the play again.
I hate having to read surtitles.
I hate to break things up ...
Other verbs: love, prefer, start

12 In pairs. How do you feel about these situations? Use the different verbs shown in the grammar box to express your feelings and reactions.

EXAMPLE:

CORNELIA: *I hate my mother chatting to my friends.*

STEFAN: *I don't mind.*

1 your mother chats to your friends
2 you read a book for school
3 you run into a teacher in a shop
4 your best friend gets angry
5 you don't get homework

13 Which two things do you:

1 detest your best friend doing?
2 avoid doing?
3 imagine doing when you are older?
4 postpone doing?
5 resent doing?

Writing

Written dialogues attempt to reproduce the characteristics of conversations (repetition, false starts, pauses, sudden changes of topic, expressions of surprise, attention getters, fillers).

The speaker is indicated at the beginning of each speech (usually in capital letters), followed by a colon (:).

14 Read the scene from Ionesco's play *The Lesson* in the 'theatre of the absurd' tradition. How does the author convey and exaggerate the characteristics of spoken language? Answer the questions.

1 What examples are there of sudden changes of topic?
2 What 'filler' is used?
3 How are pauses indicated?
4 What examples are there of false starts?
5 Why are things repeated?
6 Is the lesson a logical one?
7 Do you find the scene funny?

Main characters of the play
The Professor, *between fifty and sixty years old*
The Girl Pupil, *eighteen*
5 *years old*

Story so far: At the beginning of the play, the pupil is a bright girl who wants to work for her
10 *'Doctor's Degree' which will take place 'in three weeks'. Then she starts complaining about toothache, but the professor shows no*
15 *sympathy. As the play goes on, she 'will become more and more tired and sleepy', 'more and more passive'.*

Scene: The old Professor's study, which is also his dining-room.
20 *To the rear and slightly to the left there is a window hung with plain curtains, and outside, on the sill, pots of common or garden flowers. Three chairs round the table, two more on either side of the window, a light wallpaper, a few shelves holding books.*

25 PROFESSOR: … How, for example, would you say, in English, the roses of my grandmother are as yellow as my grandfather who was born in Asia?
PUPIL: Toothache! Toothache! Toothache!
PROFESSOR: Come along now, that doesn't stop you saying it!
30 PUPIL: In English?
PROFESSOR: In English.
PUPIL: Er … you want me to say in English: the roses of my grandmother are …
PROFESSOR: … as yellow as my grandfather who was born
35 in Asia …
PUPIL: Well then, one would say, in English, I think: the roses … of my … How do you say grandmother in English?
PROFESSOR: In English? Grandmother.
PUPIL: The roses of my grandmother … yellow, in English, you
40 say yellow?
PROFESSOR: Yes, of course!
PUPIL: Are as yellow as my grandfather when he lost his temper.
PROFESSOR: No! Who was born …
PUPIL: In Asia … I've got toothache.

15 Write a short sketch or scene from a play. Include a description of the characters and of the scene. Indicate the speaker at the beginning of each speech and don't forget the colon (:).

Get better soon

1 Match the words and the pictures.

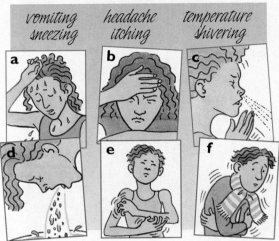

| vomiting sneezing | headache itching | temperature shivering |

a   b   c

d   e   f

Which of the above are symptoms of flu? Check your answers in the leaflet. Were you right?

2 Read the leaflet again. Mark the sentences T (true) or F (false).

When you have flu:
1 antibiotics are not the answer.
2 you can go out.
3 it is not necessary to stay in bed.
4 it is very important to keep warm.
5 you have to drink a lot of liquids.
6 it is not a good idea to take aspirin.
7 it is important to eat a lot.
8 always consult a doctor.

What to do about winter bugs

You're feeling weak and shivery, you have a headache. You sneeze again and again or have a runny nose. You may have a cough. You've got a temperature. You have lost your appetite and you're feeling sick.

You've probably got flu

There is no quick cure. You mustn't take antibiotics. Flu – influenza – is caused by a virus, and viruses do not respond to antibiotics. Taking them will only decrease the amount of vitamin C in your body.

A bout of flu may last from 24 hours to several days. Here's what to do:

- You must stay indoors. You don't have to stay in bed unless you have got a high temperature, but you have to keep warm.

- You should keep away from other members of your family as much as possible so you don't pass on the infection.

- Have plenty of drinks: water, tea, fruit juice, milky drinks.

- If your temperature is over 38°C and you have aches and pains, you ought to take two soluble aspirin or paracetamol tablets every 4 hours. You don't have to stay in bed, but you may want to.

- Try to have three light meals a day. You shouldn't force yourself to eat if you've lost your appetite.

You needn't call the doctor unless the flu persists for more than a few days or suddenly gets worse.

At the same time, you need to be aware of other diseases like meningitis. If there is any drowsiness or neck stiffness, a doctor must be contacted immediately.

Grammar

From obligation to prohibition

1 Obligation
You **must** stay indoors.
You **have to** keep warm.
You **need to** have a hospital test.

2 Advice or recommendation
You **should** keep away from other members of your family.
You **ought to** take two soluble aspirin every 4 hours.
You **shouldn't/oughtn't to** force yourself to eat if you've lost your appetite.

3 No obligation
You **don't have to** stay in bed unless you've got a high temperature.
You **needn't** call the doctor unless the flu persists.

4 Prohibition
You **mustn't** take antibiotics.

Look!
'Must' often indicates that it is the speaker who decides that something is obligatory; with 'have to', it doesn't matter who decides.
'Oughtn't to' is not used very often.

3 Choose the correct alternative.

To have a perfect health day:

1 You mustn't/don't have to leap out of bed. Your joints swell at night so you are vulnerable to injury. Stretch out first.
2 You should/shouldn't have a shower rather than a bath; the jets of water boost energy.
3 You must/mustn't have breakfast. Studies have shown it is the most important meal of the day. Without it you make more mistakes and work more slowly and less creatively.
4 Repeat an affirmation to yourself, such as 'It's a good day for me' every morning. Whatever phrase you choose, it has to/mustn't be in the present tense to make it more powerful.
5 You shouldn't/needn't watch much TV. An evening in front of the TV allows your brain to be passive and reduces your cognitive skills.
6 You ought to/have to eat your evening meal at least three hours before going to bed. That way, you can digest the food properly.
7 You need to/mustn't sleep at least eight hours a night. Surveys show that two-thirds of people don't get enough sleep.

Word watch

★ **Aches and pains** is a fixed phrase.
The words **ache** and **pain** are used to form several different compound nouns·

Aches

a headache/headaches

toothache

stomach-ache

earache

back-ache

But, a sore throat

sore eyes

Pains

knee pain

joint pain

countable

uncountable

4 Complete the sentences with one of the compound nouns in the word watch box.

1 Nine out of ten _____ are due to stress and fatigue in the head and neck muscles.
2 Wearing a support bandage can protect you against _____.
3 If you have _____, you probably need to go to the dentist.
4 Some air travellers get _____ when the plane is taking off or landing. This is because of changes of pressure in the cabin.
5 When you get _____, it can be difficult to swallow hard food such as toast.
6 Don't eat unripe apples. They might give you _____.
7 Wearing glasses that aren't strong enough can give you _____.

Get talking

5 ▭ Listen to the conversation. Tom's in bed with flu. His father, mother and little sister want to make him feel better. Who offers him:

1 some biscuits?
2 an aspirin?
3 something to read?
4 some orange juice?
5 some ice cream?

6 Which of these phrases are used to:

- make an offer?
- accept the offer?
- refuse the offer?

1 Shall I bring you …?
2 That would be great. Thanks.
3 Do you want me to get you …?
4 Thanks, but I don't really feel like …ing.
5 Why don't I bring you …?
6 I can bring you some … if you want.
7 No, thanks. I don't feel like …ing.
8 Can I bring you something …?

7 Listen again. Does Tom trust his little sister? How do you know?

8 Form groups of 3–4 for this role play. One of you has got flu. The rest ask how you are and offer to do things to help you. You accept or refuse the offers.

EXAMPLE:

MIRCEA: *How are you feeling, Sanda?*

SANDA: *I've still got a headache but I'm a bit better, thanks.*

MIRCEA: *Shall I bring you a blanket? You have to keep warm.*

SANDA: *Thanks, Mircea. I'm warm enough.*

Reading

9 Skim the article. What is it about? What is the introduction about?

10 Read the introductory paragraphs. Answer the questions.

1 Where was Marion?
2 What happened to her there?
3 Why did it happen?
4 What was done about it?

11 Choose the most suitable subtitle for each part of the article. The first one has been done as an example.

1 How does the immune system work?
2 What can you be allergic to?
3 Why do some people get allergies and not others?
4 What is an allergy?
5 What does histamine do?
6 What are the symptoms of allergy?
7 Why has allergy increased?
8 How does an allergic reaction occur?

12 Study the Grammar box opposite. Now write two passive versions of each of the following sentences.

1 They gave Nick a powerful new antibiotic.
2 Someone sent Tammy a very good book on allergies.
3 They have offered Mary the job.
4 They paid the victim compensation.
5 Her parents left Amy a large fortune.

The ene

I T WAS A GREAT PARTY. Marion and Jude took a break from dancing and went to get a snack. The lemonade was cold, the peanuts were lovely and salty. It was then that Marion started feeling sick, she couldn't breathe. She gasped for air, 5 tried to hold onto Jude's arm and fell to the ground, unconscious.

The ambulance arrived in minutes and Marion was taken to hospital. Once there, she was quickly examined and given an adrenaline injection which saved her life. She was given the 10 diagnosis: she had had an extreme allergic reaction to the peanuts.

The peanuts?! This wasn't the first time she'd had peanuts! She couldn't believe it..., until allergies were explained to her.

Allergies have become more common over the last 30 years. 15 One third of us are affected by an allergy at some point in our lives.

a) What is an allergy?

Allergy is a reaction that occurs when your immune sytem has an odd and unnecessary reaction to something which should 20 be harmless, such as pollen or peanuts.

b)

Your immune system protects the body from outside attackers – micro-organisms like viruses and bacteria. It remembers the micro-organisms and sends antibodies to attack them 25 whenever it meets them again. With an allergy, your immune system forms antibodies against harmless substances because it mistakenly believes them to be dangerous.

c)

Sometimes you can happily eat 30 or sniff something for years and then suddenly become allergic to it. The first time your immune system recognises an allergen, it makes an anti-35 body called immunoglobulin E, or IgE. The IgE attaches itself to mast cells, located in the nose, mouth, throat and gastro-intestinal tract. When the body 40 is exposed to the allergen again, the IgE attacks the intruders and destroys them. As this happens, the surface of the mast cells is broken and 45 histamine is released into the body.

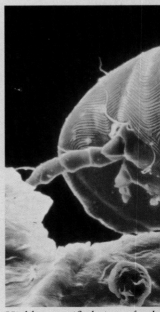

Highly magnified view of a dus

y within

d)

Histamine makes blood vessels widen, fluids leak into the tissues and muscles go into spasm. This leads to the symptoms of allergy. 50

e)

The symptoms vary from rashes, itchy skin, sore eyes, vomiting, diarrhoea and breathlessness. The most severe allergic reaction is often triggered by peanuts. There may be such a bad swelling in the back of the neck that the sufferer 55 cannot breathe; and such a rapid drop in blood pressure that (s)he loses consciousness, as happened to Marion. The symptoms can be reduced with antihistamines, but allergies are difficult to treat.

f)

You can have an allergic reaction to almost anything: pollen, 60 insect stings, eggs, fish, nuts, dairy products, citrus fruits, certain cereals, coffee, dust mite droppings, pet fur, domestic chemicals, some medicines like penicillin – the list goes on!

g)

Allergies run in families. The ability to make lots of IgE is 65 passed from parents to children.

h)

There are many theories, but most experts believe the increase in allergies is because of changes in our lifestyle and 70 environment. We are exposed to more allergens because we

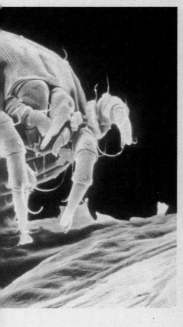

eat more processed foods, keep more pets indoors, and live in warmer houses – the dust mites' favourite 75 environment!

There may also be a link between allergies and the great advantages of modern life, such as antibiotics, 80 clean modern homes and generally less disease. Once our immune systems were kept busy fighting off disease, now they've got less 85 to do and so may direct their energies against less harmful substances like pollen. In other words, they have become over-sensitive. 90

Grammar

Passives with two objects

Remember we use the passive voice when the agent is not known or when the action is more important.

They **examined** her.
She **was examined**.

1 *Some verbs (e.g.* send, give, tell) *have two objects. They can be written with or without the preposition* to.

They gave **her the diagnosis**.
They gave **the diagnosis to her**.

When you use these verbs in the passive, either object can become the subject of the new sentence.

She was given **the diagnosis**.
The diagnosis was given **to her**.

2 *A few verbs with two objects (e.g.* explain, expose) *always use a preposition for the second object.*

They explained allergies **to her**. ✓
Allergies were explained **to her**. ✓
~~She was explained allergies.~~ ✗

Look!

New or important information usually comes at the end of the passive sentence.

(What was Nick given?)
Nick was given **an antibiotic**.

(Who was given the antibiotic?)
The antibiotic was given to **Nick**.

13 **Have you ever been given these medicines? If so, when? Tell a partner.**

EXAMPLE:
I've been given aspirin before.
I was given aspirin when I had a headache.

- aspirin
- insulin
- antibiotics
- antihistamines

Revision

1 Are you an optimist or a pessimist?

a) Look at this picture of a glass of water. Choose sentence A or B, to label the picture.

A The glass is half-full.
B The glass is half-empty.

b) Now read the dictionary definitions. Which word is represented by A above, and which by B?

2 Skim this article. Answer these questions.

1 What kind of text does the article probably come from?
2 What is the likely purpose of the article?
3 What would be a good title for the article?

op.ti.mism ('ɒptɪ'mɪẑm) *n* a tendency to give more attention to the good side of a situation or to expect the best possible result.

pes.si.mism ('pəsɪ'mɪẑm) *n* a tendency to give more attention to the bad side of a situation or to expect the worst possible result.

Mariam and Rosalie are best friends. They are both gifted musicians and have been preparing for an audition to
5 join a Youth Orchestra. 'I know the jury are difficult to please, so I've been working hard,' says Mariam enthusiastically. 'I have to feel confident and I mustn't allow myself
10 to contemplate failing at the last moment. Anyway, the way I see it, I've already achieved something: I've become a better violinist!'

Rosalie is not so optimistic. 'I've
15 been losing sleep over the audition. If I fail, I may not be given another chance,' she explains anxiously. 'I've been practising for weeks, but deep down I feel I've been wasting
20 my time. I can't imagine the orchestra wanting me when they've got so much choice! I mustn't get my hopes up.'

We don't know which of the girls
25 will succeed but we can guess who is likely to be the ultimate winner in this situation.

What is optimism?

Optimism is the ability to see the
30 positive side of things rather than the negative. Optimistic thinkers, like Mariam, are usually positive people because they approach life with the expectation that a happy outcome is
35 both desirable and possible. True optimism doesn't mean being unaware of problems; it means actively looking for the positive factors in a situation.

40 Why is optimism useful?

Seeing the positive side of difficult circumstances gives optimists the courage and ability to carry on and try again. They can learn from their
45 mistakes and are able to apply that knowledge at a later stage. Pessimists, on the other hand, tend either to avoid similar situations in the future, or to repeat the same
50 fatalistic errors.

Optimists focus on what they have achieved rather than on what might have been. They also have a much broader definition of success
55 than pessimists, and take any sign of progress as evidence of achievement.

You too can become an optimist

Some people seem to be born
60 optimists, but if you are not one of them, it is never too late to achieve
65 an optimistic outlook on life. Here is how you can do it:

◆ *Focus on your successes and minimise your failures.*

70 Start by taking pleasure in your successes, however small. Don't think that you have just been lucky and that your success won't last. Instead, acknowledge that you have
75 only your own effort and ability to thank.

◆ *Look for positive features, then focus on solutions.*

As the saying goes: 'Every cloud
80 has a silver lining'. This means that some good can come out of a negative experience. Adopt the PIN code: first look for something *positive* about the situation; next, look for something *interesting* in it.
85 Then and only then, look for the *negatives*. Work out what went wrong and think of what you must do differently in future.

◆ *Adopt broad-minded attitudes.*

90 Your family has been ignoring you a bit. Do you automatically think: 'Nobody cares about me …'? Don't jump to conclusions! A broad-minded attitude would be to look for
95 other reasons why they are behaving that way towards you. Think instead: 'They probably have problems of their own. It's nothing personal, and it will pass.'

3 Scan the text to find the following information. Make notes.

1 a definition of optimism
2 the advantages of having an optimistic outlook
3 ways to develop optimism
4 an example of a narrow-minded attitude

4 Write the words from text that show:

1 the girls' recent activity.
2 the importance of the audition for Mariam.
3 the importance of the audition for Rosalie.
4 Rosalie's anxiety about the audition.
5 Rosalie's pessimistic attitude towards her efforts.
6 Mariam's positive attitude towards her efforts.

EXAMPLE: 1 *They have been preparing for an audition.*

5 Rosalie has failed the audition. You are her music teacher. Write a list of suggestions to help her react optimistically. Use information from the text and verbs to express obligation, advice and prohibition.

EXAMPLE: *You mustn't give up.*

6 Find these nouns in the text.

> optimism   jury   outcome   situation
> orchestra   experience   family

Which are collective nouns? Are they regarded as a single unit, or a group of individuals? How do you know? Underline the word(s) in the text which helped you decide.

UNIT A EXERCISE 13 STUDENT A
a) Describe this picture to your partner.
b) Draw the picture your partner describes to you. Ask for clarification if necessary.

Listening

7 You are going to hear an excerpt from *The Little Prince*, a book by Antoine de Saint-Exupéry, about a mysterious little prince from another planet. In this excerpt, the little prince meets a fox during his visit to Earth. Listen to their conversation.

a) Answer these questions.
 1 Has the little prince ever seen a fox before? How do we know?
 2 Has the little prince ever heard the word 'tame' before? How do we know?
 3 What does 'to tame' mean, according to the fox?
 4 Does the little prince trust the fox? How do we know?

b) What does the fox think about these topics? Listen again and make a note of the words that helped you answer.
 1 Men in general
 2 How one can make friends
 3 Men and friendship
 4 The value of words

8 What are the fox's opinions about men? Do you think he is optimistic, pessimistic, or just realistic? Do you agree with his opinions?

Why (not)? Discuss this with your partner. Don't forget to ask for clarification if you don't understand your partner's points.

Project

9 In groups, plan a quiz to find out whether the people in your class are optimistic or pessimistic.

a) Write 8–10 questions about different topics (for example, the future, the environment, the world, etc.) Offer two possible answers, one optimistic, one pessimistic.

 EXAMPLE: *When you finish your studies, how easy do you think it will be to find a good job?*

 ☐ *Easy*   ☐ *Difficult*

b) Distribute your quiz to people in your class and ask them to answer it.
c) Analyse your results: what kind of things are people in your class optimistic/pessimistic about?

Grammar practice

10 Complete this letter with the correct form of the verbs in brackets. Use the Present Perfect or the Present Perfect Continuous. (Unit A)

Dear Mariana,

I loved your letter. It really made me laugh. It sounds like you _have been having_ (**1** have) a wonderful time. Not me!

I_____ (**1** read) a very good book. It's called 'Of Mice and Men'. I ____ really ____ (**2** enjoy) reading the book but now I have to write an essay about it: to what extent is 'Of Mice and Men' an optimistic story?! I _____ (**3** sit) in front of an empty page for hours but I _____ (**4** not make) any progress. I _____ (**5** write) the first sentence five times but I can't think of anything to say. I_____ (**6** beg) my brainy sister her to help me all week; I ____ even _____ (**7** offer) to do her chores for a week! One day she says she will help, the next day she says she won't. I ____ seriously ____ (**8** think) of offering to lend her my blades, and you know they are my most precious possession. So, is 'Of Mice and Men' optimistic? I don't know – I'm certainly not!

Love,

Karina

11 Write a suitable form of the verb *to be* in the line blanks (_____) and a suitable pronoun in the dotted blanks (.........). (Unit A)

It's funny how different the children in a family (1) _____ even when (2) .... are brought up in the same way. My older sister, for example, is always involved in things in our community. (3) .... (4) _____ very grateful, of course, but my family (5) _____ a little worried that she's trying to do too much. I, on the other hand, don't enjoy being with lots of people. Once, I was part of a committee to organise social activities at school. What a mistake! The committee (6) _____ so unhappy with my work that (7) .... suggested I joined a different group. The new group (8) _____ in charge of organising the school library. This was just my cup of tea and (9) .... were very happy with my work.

Finally, there is my five-year-old little sister. She's a great actress and needs an audience: the bigger the audience, (10) _____, the happier she is! I guess with two sisters like mine, I will have to get used to being with people.

12 Put the adverbials in brackets in the correct position to complete the sentences. Write out the complete sentences. (Unit B)

1	*Of Mice and Men* is set	(in the 1930s/ in California)
2	The book was written by John Steinbeck	(beautifully)
3	I read the book	(at school/ last year/ very fast)
4	It is about George and Lennie, two farm workers looking for work	(in California/during the depression/in different ranches)
5	They dream of working for themselves	(one day/in a ranch of their own)
6	The story ends when George shoots Lennie	(tragically/ by 'the deep green pool of the Salinas river')

13 Complete these sentences with the correct form, infinitive or gerund, of the verbs in the box. (Unit B)

choose   read (x2)   understand   have to discuss   become   study   understand (don't)

I enjoy (1) ____ books very much. I prefer (2) ____ in my own language but last year, at school, we started (3)____ books in English, which I really like. I don't mind (4) ____ every word and I hate (5) ____ look words up in the dictionary. I like most kinds of books but I can't imagine (6) ____ to read a love story for pleasure. I love (8) ____ books with other students. I would like (9) _____ a critic one day.

UNIT A EXERCISE 13 STUDENT B

a) Draw the picture your partner is going to describe to you. Ask for clarification if necessary.

b) Describe the picture opposite to your partner

14 The students in a class below you have just started reading books in English. Write a pamphlet to help them to read in English more easily. Use your own knowledge and the verbs below. (Unit C)

> must(n't)   (don't) have to   need to
> should(n't)   ought to   needn't

Reading in English: how to succeed

EXAMPLE: *You should always try to predict what is in the text.*

15 Rewrite these sentences. Put the parts underlined into the passive. (Unit C)

EXAMPLE: *1 Mariam is worried that she won't be given a second chance.*

1 Mariam is worried that <u>they won't give her a second chance</u>.
2 Patsy won a competition. <u>They gave her a book as a prize</u>.
3 I forgot to return my library book and <u>they have sent me a warning</u>.
4 <u>The teacher just told us that there is a test next week</u>.
5 When I was sick <u>people brought me lots of magazines to read</u>.
6 I didn't know anything about poetry but <u>they taught me how to appreciate it at school</u>.
7 <u>They explained different rhyme schemes to me</u>.
8 I am a good reader because <u>they exposed me to books as a child</u>.

CHISWICK PARK

Grammar

1 talk about events in the past and their relevance to present situations using the Present Perfect. (Unit A)
2 emphasise the duration of events which continue up to the present using the Present Perfect Continuous. (Unit A)
3 use collective nouns correctly. (Unit A)
4 order different kinds of adverbials in a sentence correctly. (Unit B)
5 use a variety of verbs followed by the gerund. (Unit B)
6 talk about degrees of obligation and prohibition using a variety of modal verbs. (Unit C)
7 use the passive voice with two objects. (Unit C)

Skills

READING

- skim a text to identify its organisation and its main ideas. (Unit A)
- scan a text to find specific information. (Unit B)

WRITING

- plan, organise and write a composition. (Unit A)
- write natural-sounding dialogues. (Unit B)

LISTENING

- use different strategies to understand conversations more easily. (Unit B)

SPEAKING

- ask for clarification when you don't understand and clarify your own message. (Unit A)
- issue an invitation, accept and refuse an invitation from others. (Unit B)
- offer help, accept and refuse offers from others. (Unit C)
- ask and give information about health. (Unit C)
- express trust. (Unit C)

Crossing borders

1 In pairs, write a list of countries where English is an official language. Write notes on the things you know about the countries on your list.

EXAMPLE: *Great Britain – several countries (England, Scotland, Wales), rains a lot*

Now compare your information with another pair.

2 Imagine you had to emigrate to one of the countries in Exercise 1. Find out your partner's answers to these questions.

1 Which country would you most like to emigrate to?
2 Why have you chosen that country?
3 What things would you find difficult?
4 What do you think your parents would find difficult?

Reading

Articles often include a short introductory paragraph. This paragraph will help you predict what kind of article you are going to read (serious and formal or light and entertaining). Then you can decide if you want to read the article.

3 Read these alternative introductory paragraphs. Are the articles introduced going to be serious and formal or light and entertaining?

1
Since the fall of Communism, many residents of the former Communist bloc have headed for different countries. Some have been given permission to stay. Natalie Napier reports on the adaptation of an immigrant family to their host country.

2
How would you feel if you had to go and live in another country? Natalie Napier reports on a brother and sister who have made the most of it.

3
'We're beginning to do things the English way. We even went to Spain on holiday this year!' Natalie Napier talks to a brother and sister who have made the most of their new country.

Read the article and check your response to number 3

The new speakers of English

'We're beginning to do things the English way. We even went to Spain on holiday this year!' Natalie Napier talks to a brother and sister who have made the most of their new country.

Four years after she and her family arrived in Britain from Poland with
5 only some English, eighteen-year-old Joasia Kossowska has been accepted by Cambridge University to read law. Her younger brother Piotr, fifteen, has won a scholarship to a public school. He has been visiting museums all summer: his ambition is to become an artist.

When the family emigrated to Britain, Joasia and Piotr went to a
10 local school. For the first year they had to have special English classes but within a year they were overtaking their fellow pupils.

'When we left Poland I was attending *Szkoła Podstawowa*, that's sort of like secondary school in Britain. I had done Russian for three years but didn't know very much English,' says Joasia. 'When we
15 started the English lessons I studied the same way I had studied Russian. You know, grammar exercises, lists of words. But I also had to talk, talk, talk from the start. I needed to make friends!'

'And we had to do lots of interpreting for my parents,' adds Piotr. 'They really had problems speaking English. Once, my mother asked
20 for "roast kitchen" in a restaurant. It took the waitress a while to work out that she wanted chicken!' he laughs. 'But they've made a lot of progress since then!'

Language problems aside, has adapting to a new country been difficult? 'A bit,' says Joasia. Some things were puzzling. 'The first
25 time I heard about hockey I thought it must be on ice. I'd been to several games back in Poland. It was always men who played, too. So I was surprised to be taken to a field, but when I saw that *girls* were playing on *grass* I was flabbergasted!'

Piotr thinks they have adapted well. 'We've been living here in
30 England for four years now and we're beginning to do things the English way. We even went to Spain on holiday this year!' he says with a smile.

4 Read the article again. Which paragraph (2–7):

1 focuses on Joasia's language learning?
2 talks about Joasia and Piotr's future?
3 makes a link with the introduction?
4 is about the parents' language learning?
5 deals with the adaptation process?
6 is about Joasia and Piotr's early progress?

5 Look at your answers to Exercise 2 again. Are any of them similar to Joasia and Piotr's experiences?

Grammar

6 Underline the past tenses in the text. Match them with the explanations in the grammar box.

Talking about the past

Present Perfect
Piotr **has won** a scholarship.
We don't know when.

They **have made** a lot of progress.
And they will probably make more.

Present Perfect Continuous
They **have been living** here for four years.
That seems quite a long time.

Past Simple
They **emigrated** four years ago.
Completed action. We know when it happened.

Past Continuous
I saw that girls **were playing** on grass.
They started before she arrived and then continued.

When we left Poland I **was attending** *Szkoła Podstawowa.*
She attended until they left Poland.

Past Perfect
They **had studied** Russian before they came here.
'Had studied' is the earlier action.

Need more help? Go to pages 111 and 112.

---

7 Put the verb in brackets in the correct tense. In some cases there is more than one possible answer.

1 Many people from the former Communist bloc _____ (emigrate) to other countries since the end of Communism. The Kossowskis _____ (leave) Poland four years ago.
2 When the reporter _____ (arrive) at the Kossowskis' house, they _____ (have) tea so they offered her some.
3 Mrs Kossowska _____ (study) English for several years. Her English is quite good now but she doesn't want to give up her lessons yet.
4 Joasia and Piotr _____ (not study) English very much before they _____ (arrive) in England. Their schooling _____ (be) in Polish.
5 Piotr _____ (attend) an English school for almost half of his school life. His next two years at school will also be in English.
6 The Kossowskis _____ (not, be) to Britain before they _____ (move) there. It was their first time in the country.
7 Piotr _____ (go) to a Polish school for six years.

Listening

✦ *Knowing what sort of listening material you are going to hear helps you understand it because you can predict its structure and content.*

8 You are going to listen to a seventeen-year-old called Richard. Look at this and answer the questions.

BBC World Service
Programmes broadcast overnight on Radio 4 LW (198kHz)
1.00 World News. **1.09** British News.
1.15 Outlook. **1.30** The Young Internationals – Victoria Marr talks to young people about their experiences of emigration. **2.10** Short Story: *Sticky Carpet* by Frank Rowan.

1 What sort of text are you going to listen to?
2 What structure will the programme have, do you think? A report, a monologue by Richard or an interview?
3 Write a list of at least five things you think will be mentioned.

🎧 **Now listen to the broadcast and check your answers.**

9 **Listen again. Complete the notes that summarise what Richard says.**

1 emigrated to Argentina . . .
2 mother born there and wanted . . .
3 Richard couldn't stay with father: . . .
4 parents felt better if Richard . . .
5 Richard found classes strange at first: . . .
6 had never . . .
7 hopes . . .
8 misses . . .

Listen to the tape again and check your answers.

Writing

⬥ *Articles are usually organised like this:*
1 Introductory paragraph: to attract the readers' attention.
2 Development paragraphs: each on a different point.
3 Concluding paragraph: rounds off the article and is often linked to the introductory paragraph.

10 **You are a journalist. Use your notes from Exercise 9 to write a short article about Richard for a teenage magazine.**

Reading

11 **Look at the introductory paragraph of the following article. Write three sentences on what you think the article is about. Then read the article and check your sentences.**

12 **A friend of yours wants to know about the Global Schoolhouse project. Complete the dialogue with information from the text. Use your own words as far as possible.**

FRIEND: What's a video conference?
YOU: It's . . .
FRIEND: Oh! Have you ever heard of something called the Global Schoolhouse project? Doesn't it have something to do with videos?
YOU: Yes. I read about it in *High Flyer*, our English book. It's . . .
FRIEND: That sounds fun! But I don't understand how they do it. What equipment do they have to use?
YOU: . . . but don't ask me how exactly it all works!
FRIEND: And can the people see and hear each other clearly?
YOU: Well, in the session described in the book . . . but apparently it didn't matter.
FRIEND: And what sort of things do they talk about?
YOU: The conference in the book was about . . . but they . . .
FRIEND: Wouldn't it be nice if we had the same in our school?
YOU: (*Give your opinion!*) . . .

So near, yet so far apart

Dennis McCaffrey joins British pupils in a high-tech transatlantic classroom. The lesson today is a video conference with students on
5 *the other side of the world.*
'Are you there, London, England?'
   'Yes,' said Sarah, making her first transatlantic video appearance at the age of fourteen. The images of
10 Sarah and other English pupils were appearing in classrooms in Tennessee, Virginia and California, USA. Each group could see themselves, and the others, on a
15 quartered computer screen.
   It was the first session of the Global Schoolhouse project, using inexpensive new technology for a video conference between schools
20 thousands of miles apart. The transmission wasn't very clear but nobody seemed to mind: it was clear enough to follow the gist of what was said.
25 Teachers present on both sides of the Atlantic were very impressed. Nothing went wrong and the pupils behaved like experienced professionals. 'We had told them not to
30 waste time,' said one of the teachers involved. 'And they didn't. They immediately got down to the subject of the conference, water pollution.'

The conversation was at times
35 very serious. 'The sooner we can work together, the sooner the problems will be solved,' an English girl said. At other times, however, it was more mundane. An English
40 boy asked the Californians about *Baywatch*, the TV series about lifeguards. 'The water is never as clean as it looks on TV!' answered David from Jefferson High.
45 'Didn't you get nervous?' we asked Sarah afterwards. 'Oh, yes,' she said. 'I went bright red and felt very hot. I'd never talked to

Grammar

Negative statements

Remember:

1 *Clauses without an auxiliary verb take the correct form of* do not *plus the infinitive.*
The children **didn't waste** any time.

2 *Infinitive structures do not need* do.
They told the children **not to waste** any time.

3 *Two negative words in the same clause are almost always incorrect.*
I ~~**didn't never**~~ **talk** to them.✗
I **never talked** to them.✓
No, I **never talked** to them.✓

4 Nobody, nothing *and other* no-*words are emphatic so at other times we use* not . . . anybody/thing/where, *etc.*
They **didn't** do **anything** wrong.

5 Nobody, no one *and* nothing *are often used at the beginning of a sentence.*
Nothing went wrong.

Negative questions

Generally used to express surprise, disbelief or when we expect a yes *answer.*

Informal	Formal
auxiliary + n't + *subject* + *verb*	*auxiliary* + *subject* + not + *verb*
Didn't you get nervous?	**Did** you **not** get nervous?

---

13 **These examples of students' work are wrong. Write them correctly without changing the words underlined.**

EXAMPLE: 1 *The pupils never behaved badly.*

1 The pupils didn't never <u>behaved badly</u>.
2 One girl <u>didn't know</u> nobody in the States.
3 Most people had <u>never</u> seen nothing like it.

4 <u>Nobody</u> did nothing wrong.
5 There <u>isn't</u> nobody in the computer room.
6 Dave doesn't never <u>swims</u> in the sea.

7 I <u>haven't</u> been nowhere in the last week.
8 <u>It's important</u> to don't panic.
9 Have not you done your <u>homework</u>?

14 **Imagine you are going to take part in the Global Schoolhouse project.**

a) Make a list of four possible topics for a video conference. Then make a list of four countries you would like to have the video conference with. Make a note of your reasons.
EXAMPLE:
Topics: the environment, sports . . .
Countries: Britain – interested in the country
*   the United States – very good at sports*

b) In groups of three or four, you must choose **one** of the countries and **one** of the topics on your lists. Use your notes in a) and give your group your opinion.

c) Make a list of questions you would ask the people in the country of your choice about the topic you have chosen.
EXAMPLE: *Country: the United States Topic: sports*
Do you play different sports at different times of the year?

d) Swap your group work with other groups. What were the most popular topics and countries?

anybody in the States through a
50 computer.'
    'I'd talked to no one in the States, full stop,' commented another girl.
    The Global Schoolhouse project uses video cameras and personal
55 computers linked to the Internet, an international network. The aim of the project as a whole is to increase young people's awareness of other cultures. Forty countries
60 have so far participated in the scheme. The future looks exciting – there is no reason why more schools right across the globe can't talk to others like this.

Exploring the world

1 Look at the advertisement. Answer the questions.

1 What does it advertise?
2 What is it about?
3 How much does it cost?
4 Where is Ranulph Fiennes from?

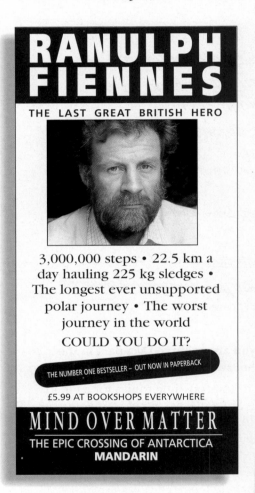

RANULPH FIENNES

THE LAST GREAT BRITISH HERO

3,000,000 steps • 22.5 km a day hauling 225 kg sledges • The longest ever unsupported polar journey • The worst journey in the world
COULD YOU DO IT?

THE NUMBER ONE BESTSELLER – OUT NOW IN PAPERBACK

£5.99 AT BOOKSHOPS EVERYWHERE

MIND OVER MATTER
THE EPIC CROSSING OF ANTARCTICA
MANDARIN

2 The advertisement asks, 'Could you do it?' Make a list of things which you think would make an expedition like Fiennes's across Antarctica very difficult.

EXAMPLE: *It is very cold in Antarctica.*

Reading

3 Read the book extract. Which four difficulties does it mention? Are any of them on your list?

Science has learnt a great deal from polar expeditions. For instance, we now know a lot more about the effects polar conditions have on a person's mind and body.

5 In the early days, explorers often went mad. One cause of this madness was later discovered: when people aren't used to living in extreme cold, their bodies use up a lot of energy to keep warm and this gets rid of all the vitamins in the body. The brain, deprived of vitamins, can't work normally, at least until the body gets used to the cold. After a certain period, the body adapts itself
10 to its new environment and makes the most of whatever vitamins are available.

The time spent in total darkness also has a negative effect on people's minds. Winter in polar regions is characterised by permanent night and lasts several months. Human beings are not
15 used to spending long periods of time in the dark. In northern latitudes people get depressed during the dark winter months. Now we know that this depression – known as SAD (Seasonal Affective Disorder) – can be reduced by the use of sun lamps.

Low temperatures can cause any part of the body to freeze. This
20 painful condition is called frostbite. Although the body does get used to functioning in low temperatures, the danger of frostbite is always there if temperatures fall below freezing point. Nowadays, polar explorers carry medication which they can take to allow the blood to flow and slowly defrost the affected parts.
25 Another common disorder is altitude sickness. The ice is sometimes more than three kilometres thick, which makes Antarctica one of the highest regions in the world. At that altitude there is little oxygen, so headaches, vomiting and dehydration – the symptoms of altitude sickness – are common. After about a
30 year at high altitude, the body gets used to the lack of oxygen in the air. It compensates by storing more oxygen in the blood.

4 The editor of a popular science magazine answers readers' questions. Unfortunately, her computer broke down and all her readers' questions were deleted. Luckily, she's still got the answers. Read the text again and help her rewrite the questions.

1 Because, when it is very cold, the brain doesn't get enough vitamins. Fortunately, this doesn't often happen any more.
2 Yes. It can be reduced by using sun lamps.
3 It is always a danger but these days explorers take special medication to cure it.
4 You can get headaches and you may vomit.
5 Because, although there are no mountains, the layer of ice is very thick.

Vocabulary

5 Find words in the text to match the definitions.

1 To take something away from somebody.
_ _ _ □ _ □ _
2 To make something suitable for new conditions.
_ □ _ _ _
3 A long, organised journey made for a specific purpose. □ _ _ _ _ _ _ _ □ _
4 A drug used to treat an illness. _ _ _ _ _ _ □ _ _ □
5 This word describes something which hurts a lot.
_ □ _ _ _ □ _

Complete this word with the letters in the boxes and find out a quality explorers must have.

Explorers have to be _ _ _ _ _ _ U _ _ _ S.

Pronunciation

6 Read the words aloud with your partner. Which word in each group has a different stress pattern? Draw the shape of the stress patterns using a little box (□) for the unstressed syllables and a big one (□) for the stressed syllables.

☐ □ □
1 latitude   temperature   Antarctica
2 environment   expedition   medication
   □   □
3 climate   painful   extreme
4 deprive   depressed   freezing

▭ Listen and check your answers. Say the words.

Grammar

Be/get used to

1 not be used to + verb-ing
                    noun phrase

When people **aren't used to living** in extreme cold, they have health problems.
When people **aren't used to extreme cold,** they have health problems.
*People who haven't lived in very cold places have health problems because those temperature conditions are **new** and **strange** to their bodies.*

2 get used to + verb-ing
                 noun phrase

After a while, the body **gets used to functioning** in a cold climate.
After a while, the body **gets used to a cold climate.**
The body adapts to the conditions.

3 be used to + verb-ing
                noun phrase
Finally, the body **is used to functioning** in a cold climate.
Finally, the body **is used to a cold climate.**
The body has adapted to the conditions.

---

7 Read Kirsty's letter to her pen friend. Rewrite the phrases underlined using a correct form of *(not) be used to* and *get used to.*

10 Walton Street
Sydney
31st January, 1996

Dear João,
    I have just come back from a camping trip in the outback. It was a great experience once we <u>adapted to</u> conditions in the camp. The first few nights I couldn't sleep because I had never slept in a tent so I wasn't used to not having a bed! To tell you the truth, I was nervous at night because I <u>was unfamiliar with</u> the noises and I <u>had never shared</u> a room (or a tent!) with other people. (I<u>'ve always had</u> my own room at home.) But I soon <u>adapted to</u> that and we had a lot of fun in our tents.
    It was very hot during the daytime but very cold at night so I caught a cold because I <u>was not accustomed to</u> the changes in temperature. But anyway we had a great time on the trip: we saw lots of animals and studied the sky at night. Now I feel like a great explorer! The only thing I <u>never became accustomed to</u> was not having a real toilet! If you ever have a chance to visit me, you can come to the outback too.
    I'm sure you would <u>adapt to</u> life in the camp more quickly than I did!
    Take care and write soon,

        Kirsty

8 These foreign students are coming to live in your town for a few months.

a) What do you think life is like in their country? Think about the food, the weather and the general environment and write notes.
EXAMPLE: *Ella: very cold; probably small town; eats fish?*

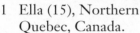

1   Ella (15), Northern Quebec, Canada.

2   David (14), Alex (15), New York City, USA.

b) What do you think they will find difficult about your country? Why? Write notes about the things each student will have to get used to.
EXAMPLE: – *used to living in a cold climate* ⟶ *will have to get used to heat.*

Writing

9 Write a letter to one of the students in Exercise 8a. Use your notes from Exercise 8b and give them tips on how to make their stay more pleasant. Use phrases like *Why don't you . . . ?, You should . . .* and *Make sure you . . .*

Reading

10 Read the poem extract. Who do you think 'the third' could be?

Who is the third who walks always beside you?

When I count, there are only you and I together

But when I look ahead up the white road

There is always another one walking beside you

From *The Waste Land* by T S Eliot

11 Read the article on page 13. Compare your guess with the information there.

12 Read the article again. Find the names of the people referred to.

1   They felt the presence of a phantom traveller.
2   He wrote the story of his journey in Antarctica.
3   He thought he'd heard spirits calling his name.
4   He was a phantom traveller himself!
5   Apart from Fletch, one other person in the text who is different from the others. (Why?)

Grammar

Clauses of concession: *even though* and *despite*

the fact that + *sentence*
1   Despite + *verb*-ing
     noun

Explorers tend to be hard-headed.
contrasts with
Many of them have sensed a ghostly companion.
⟶ **Despite the fact that** explorers tend to be hard-headed, many of them have sensed a ghostly companion.
Explorers are hard-headed so it seems surprising that they have felt the presence of a ghost.

Martin felt Fletch's presence constantly.
contrasts with
He never actually saw him.
⟶ **Despite feeling** his presence constantly, Martin never actually saw Fletch.

Shackleton's Antarctic journey was a failure.
contrasts with
His book *South* has become famous.
⟶ **Despite the failure** of Shackleton's Antarctic journey, his book has become famous.

2   Even though + *sentence*

There were only three of them.
contrasts with
They felt a 'fourth presence'.
⟶ **Even though** there were only three of them, they felt a 'fourth presence'.

Phantom travellers

Despite the fact that explorers and great travellers tend to be hard-headed and practical, many of them have sensed a ghostly companion on
5 their travels. Marco Polo was one of the first to describe this. During the thirteenth century, he crossed the Lop Nor desert on the way to China, and told the following spooky tale:
10 'When a man is riding by night through this desert and something happens to make him stop and lose touch with his companions . . . then he hears spirits talking in such a way
15 that they seem to be his companions. Sometimes, indeed, they call him by name . . . '
Other explorers have also written about this feeling. Despite the failure
20 of Ernest Shackleton's Antarctic journey – his ship broke up in the ice – the written account of it, *South*, has become famous. T S Eliot was inspired by it when he wrote *The*
25 *Waste Land*.

Shackleton wrote: 'I know that during that long march of thirty-six hours over the unnamed mountains and glaciers it often seemed to me
30 that we were four, not three.'
Explorer Steve Martin and his two team mates even made 'the fourth man' an official member of the party when they were crossing Greenland!
35 Even though there were only three men on the expedition, they felt a fourth presence who always walked to the left of the party. They called him Fletch and he even got into the
40 record books. 'It was a bit of a joke,' Martin says, 'but having a fourth member along meant you could always blame something on Fletch!' Despite feeling his presence
45 constantly, Martin never actually saw Fletch.
It is unlikely that so many serious explorers were lying. Were their minds affected by the difficult
50 conditions experienced during their travels, or could there be another, more mysterious explanation?

13 Match the sentences to make contrasting pairs of sentences.

It was very hot in the desert.

There was no vegetation in that part of the desert.

He was an experienced explorer.

She gets altitude sickness.

He knew it was a dangerous expedition.

I am very adventurous.

a) He couldn't finish the trip.

b) I wouldn't become an explorer.

c) He agreed to go on the expedition.

d) She decided to climb Mount Everest.

e) They wore heavy clothes.

f) They thought they could see palm trees in the distance.

Now join the contrasting pairs of sentences using *despite, despite the fact* or *even though.*

Get talking

14 You are part of the selection committee for a polar expedition. There is only one place left and two people have applied. Your task is to choose the best candidate for the job.

a) Unscramble the sentences to find some ways of negotiating a solution to a problem.
  1 spend time on their own/forgetting that/ explorers also/aren't you/need to/be able to/?/
  2 think/is/experience/don't/important/you/ too/that/?/
  3 you/wouldn't/that/say/important/training/is/?/
  4 good health/isn't/more important/ experience/than/?/

b) Student A: Turn to page 102.
Student B: Turn to page 105.

That's what friends are for

1 **What is a friend? Tick the definitions you agree with. Write your own definition too.**

A friend is someone . . .

1 who is always there if you need him/her.
2 who has exactly the same interests as you.
3 who listens more than he/she talks.
4 to have fun with.
5 . . . . . .

In pairs, compare answers.

2 **Read the advertisement and complete the questionnaire in it.**

3 **Work in groups. Read the fact files from Hands Across the World. Decide who would be a suitable pen friend for each of the members of your group.**

EXAMPLE:
PEDRO: *I think Sylvia should write to Benny because they both love football.*

Name: Ritsuko Takei
Age: 15
Nationality: Japanese
Notes: Wants to have pen friends who are interested in learning about other countries. Fond of dancing and very keen on music. Also likes shopping for clothes.

Name: Benny Jamieson
Age: 14
Nationality: Australian
Notes: Looking for pen friends from all over the world. Interested in all sports. Especially keen on football. Worried about the environment.

Name: Carol Andrews
Age: 15
Nationality: Canadian
Notes: Wants to write to young people from other countries. Very keen on pop music and the cinema. Shocked by violence – not afraid of speaking out against it.

HANDS ACROSS THE WORLD

Have you ever wondered what life is like in far-away countries? Well, our pen friend programme will put you in touch with people your age in many countries around the world. For just £5, you can join our organisation and make friends for life. How? Just complete the questionnaire and our computer will match you with people with the same interests and ideas as yours in countries of your choice.

Name: _____

Sex: Masc. ❏   Fem. ❏   Age: ❏   Nationality: _____
Countries where you would like to have a pen friend: _____

Tick (✔) the alternative(s) which apply to you or supply another one.

1 What are you interested in?
pop music
weird facts ❏
clothes ❏
the environment ❏
Other: _____

2 Who do you get angry with most often?
parents
teachers ❏
brothers/sisters ❏
Other: _____

3 What leisure activities are you keen on?
sport
TV ❏
reading ❏
cinema ❏
Other: _____

4 What are you afraid of?
spiders
going to the dentist ❏
the dark ❏
natural disasters
(e.g. earthquakes) ❏
wild funfair rides ❏
Other: _____

5 Which of these do you tend to find funny?
jokes
small accidents ❏
certain people ❏
yourself ❏
Other: _____

6 Who are you most often embarrassed by?
parents
friends ❏
brothers/sisters ❏
Other: _____

7 Which of these things worry you?
relationships ❏
your school marks ❏
pollution ❏
your appearance ❏
world poverty ❏
Other: _____

8 What do you find shocking?
impoliteness
violence ❏
swear words ❏
rebellious behaviour ❏
nothing ❏
Other: _____

Grammar

> **Adjective + preposition combinations**
>
> **about**
> Pam is very **worried about** her school marks.
> I am **angry about** my friend's behaviour.
>
> **at**
> I am **good at** maths.
> My pen friend's not **bad at** letter-writing.
>
> **by**
> My granny was **shocked** and **embarrassed by** my friend's bad language. My brother was quite **amused by** it.
>
> **in**
> My friend is **interested in** reading weird stories.
>
> **of**
> She isn't **afraid of** spiders but she's **terrified of** snakes.
> My parents are **fond of** saying, 'I told you so.'
>
> **on**
> Charlie is very **keen on** the cinema.
>
> **with**
> Gill got **angry with** me when I lost her pen.

4 **Rewrite the sentences using an adjective and the correct preposition. Make sure each sentence in a pair means the same.**

EXAMPLE: 1 *Hernan is good at tennis/playing tennis.*

1 Hernan plays tennis very well.
2 She finds visits to the dentist very frightening.
3 I found the story quite amusing.
4 I like Hannah.
5 What do you find most worrying?
6 My teacher finds rudeness shocking.
7 I really don't like playing basketball.
8 There's a lot of interest in the drama club in our school.

Listing

> When you listen to someone speak in English, it is important to be able to tell how they feel about the subject they are talking about. You can tell people's attitude from: 1 the words they use; 2 the way they speak, the words they emphasise; 3 the intonation they use.

5 **You are going to listen to four people talking about pen friends.**

a) 🔲 Listen. Which of these questions are all the speakers answering?
   1 Do you have a pen friend?
   2 Do you think having pen friends is a good idea?
   3 Have you ever had a pen friend?

b) Listen again. Write *1*, *2*, *3* or *4* in the blanks.
   ____ doesn't like the idea at all.
   ____ is really not sure whether he likes the idea.
   ____ definitely likes the idea of pen friends.
   ____ is not 100 per cent sure it's a good idea.

c) 🔲 Listen to these sentences from the recording. Underline the words that the speakers emphasise.
   1 Yes, it could be good but it can also be pretty boring . . .
   2 Yes. Yes, I do.
   3 Yes, I suppose it is.
   Listen again to 2 and 3. Mark the rise/fall of the speaker's voice on 'Yes' as either ` or ^ .

d) 🔲 Listen to the speakers more carefully. What reasons do they give for their opinions?

Pronunciation

6 **Listen to the mini-dialogues to find out the people's attitudes.**

a) 🔲 Listen to the way people answer. Who sounds 1 enthusiastic; 2 unsure; 3 uninterested?

b) 🔲 Repeat the conversations after the cassette.

c) 🔲 Respond to the comments you hear by saying 'Yes, it is' with the right intonation to show your attitude.

Get talking

7 **Write these expressions in the correct place in the box.**

I suppose . . .   Definitely   Not at all!
I'm not sure . . .   Yes, but . . .   Absolutely!
Certainly not

> **Expressing your attitude**
> Positive: *Definitely*, ...
> Uncertain: . . . . . . , ... , ...
> Negative: . . . . . . , ...

8 **Do you think that pen friends are a good idea? Would you pay £5 to get one? Can you think of ways of getting pen friends without paying £5?**

9 Look at the pictures in the article. What is happening in each picture? How are the different people feeling, do you think? Have you ever felt the same way? When?

Reading

10 Read the text to find the answers to these questions.

1 What is 'the green-eyed monster'?
2 What were Jon, Peter and George called? Why?
3 In what way were they different?
4 Why did they stop being friends?
5 Name two ways in which jealousy can be a good thing.
6 Name two other ways of handling jealousy.
7 Explain in your own words why jealousy is a bit like the wind.

Grammar

> **So/such...(that) introduces a result.**
>
> 1 so + *adjective* (+ that + *sentence*)
> George is **so charming (that)** everyone wants to be his friend.
> *George is very charming. As a result, everybody wants to be his friend.*
>
> 2 so + *adverb* (+ that + *sentence*)
> He plays basketball **so well (that)** he is always chosen for the school team.
>
> 3 such + a/an + *adjective* + *singular noun* (+ that + *sentence*)
> Peter is **such a good student (that)** teachers hold him up as an example.
>
> 4 such + *adjective* + *plural/uncountable noun* (+ that + *sentence*)
> They were **such good friends (that)** they became known as the 'Three Musketeers'.

Who's afraid of the green-eyed monster?

Jon, Peter and George were best friends. They met when they were very young and became inseparable. In fact, they were such good friends that they
5 became affectionately known as the 'Three Musketeers'.
  And yet, they couldn't have been more different. Jon was
10 an accomplished a t h l e t e . He played basketball so well that he
15 was chosen to play in the school team. Peter, on the other hand, was the brainy
20 one. He was such a good student that all his teachers held him up as an example to his friends. George was the funny one. He was so charming that everybody wanted to be
25 his friend.
  As they grew older, however, they began to drift apart. George often got annoyed when people admired Jon; Jon got angry when teachers talked about
30 Peter's excellent results; and Peter got fed up with girls being friendly to him hoping he would introduce them to George.
  What went wrong? Their friendship
35 was clearly struck by the green-eyed monster.

We have all experienced jealousy at some point in our lives. Have you ever felt just a little bit jealous of your
40 friend's popularity? Do you never, ever feel the tiniest bit annoyed when your parents make a fuss of your sister's accomplishments? And how did you feel when your best friend invited
45 another friend to the cinema instead of you? Don't worry if you have at times felt jealous: jealousy is not only a normal feeling, it can also be
50 positive! The origin of the word itself is a clue: jealousy comes from the Greek word *zelos*, the desire to do as well or better
55 than another person. It can encourage you to become as good as those you admire so much.
60 So, make jealousy work for you:

• **Watch those you admire.** If you're jealous of your friend's superb tennis
65 playing, watch him/her and try to improve yours.

• **Develop your own qualities.** Your friend has such long, straight hair that she could be in a shampoo
70 advertisement! Yours is short and curly. Trying to imitate her in this case can

only lead to disappointment. Instead, make a list of your own qualities and develop them. Soon, people will admire
75 *you* for more than just beautiful hair.

• **Don't worry too much about what others think of you.** At school, work for yourself, not just to please your teachers and other
80 students. Don't spoil the pleasure of your achievements because of too much jealousy of the successes of other people.

• **Talk about your feelings.** If you
85 feel your parents pay much more attention to your brother or sister, don't just sit angrily in a corner. Instead, tell them calmly how you feel.

90 • **Learn to 'share' your friends.** You can't expect your best friend to be *your*
95 friend only. Be happy that your best friend is popular with othe people but that he/she has chosen *you* as his/her specia
100 friend. And anyway, while your bes friend is out with other people he/she probably can't wait to share his/he experiences with you!

• **Remember:** jealousy can be like th
105 wind: a refreshing breeze or destructive hurricane.

II Fill in the blanks with *so*, *such*, or *such a* and words from the text.

1 Jo was *so annoyed* when her sister got a Walkman that she didn't speak to her parents for days.
2 Voitek is an ____ musician. He plays the piano ___ well that he was offered a place with a youth orchestra.
3 The weather was ____ bad that the game was cancelled. The wind was blowing ____ hard that it felt almost like a ____.
4 Melissa is ____ kind that she has never felt the ____ bit jealous of her friends' ____.
5 Your sister's boyfriend is ____ good-looking boy!
6 They're ____ good friends that they're inseparable.
7 He is ____ fantastic tennis player that everyone watches him when he plays.

I2 Read the pairs of sentences. Join them using *so*, *such* or *such a*.

EXAMPLE: 1 *She was so jealous of her sister that she felt quite guilty.*

1 She felt quite guilty. She was very jealous of her sister.
2 His sister is a very popular girl. He feels proud of her.
3 Jealousy and admiration are very common feelings. Most friends have felt them.
4 I have a lot of respect for him. Our maths teacher explains things very patiently.
5 She could sit on her hair. She had very long hair.
6 He makes everyone laugh. He's very funny.

I3 Read the problems these people have with their friends. Use the information in the text (and your own ideas!) to give them advice. Choose one and write him/her a letter of advice.

1 'Rick, my best friend, is 1.75 m. tall and a fantastic basketball player. I'm very jealous and would love to be as good as him.'
2 'My best friend went out with other people from school and she didn't ask me to go. Does this mean we aren't best friends any more?'
3 'My brother isn't very good at his schoolwork, but when he gets good marks my parents buy him presents. I always get good marks but they don't do the same for me. I think they don't love me as much as him.'

---

1 Look at the title and the picture. What sort of story do you think *Vision of Danger* is? A romantic story? A mystery? A thriller?
2 Read Episode One and answer these questions.

1 Why do some people think Anya is strange?
2 How does she decide to go to Piccadilly Circus?
3 What happens in Piccadilly Circus?

Vision of Danger

🔊 EPISODE ONE

Anya woke up with a start. She knew straight away that today would be a special day. She had that familiar feeling in her stomach – as if lots of butterflies
5 were trapped and were flapping their wings, trying to escape.

She had had that feeling just before her grandmother died and when her father was awarded a prize for his
10 research. She felt, more than knew, most things before anybody else had heard about them, perhaps even before they had actually happened. To those who didn't know her well, Anya seemed
15 strange; to those who did know her well, she was simply special.

That bright summer morning Anya felt restless and the butterflies in her stomach were growing stronger by the minute.
20 She knew from experience that it was no good fighting it: she would have to follow it.

'Mum! I've got to go out,' she announced.
25 London was extremely hot and its streets crowded. Anya walked wherever her feet took her, as if pulled by some invisible force. And still, the funny feeling in her stomach was intensifying.
30 Eventually, she reached Piccadilly Circus, which was even busier than usual.

'Shh! Take it easy,' she whispered to the feeling in her
35 stomach. 'Whatever it is, it won't be long now!'

She stopped to let the slow traffic advance before crossing the street. A coach
40 stopped right in front of her. Anya saw herself reflected in the window. Then suddenly she realised. What she was looking at was not herself,
45 but a boy, about her age, sitting in the coach. They looked at each other with equal surprise and delight.

Anya tried to call out but no sound
50 came out of her mouth. Just then, the coach moved forward and disappeared into the London traffic.

3 Why do you think Anya couldn't call out? How do you think she was feeling?
4 Now that you have read the first episode of *Vision of Danger*, do you want to change your answer to question 1? Why (not)?
5 What do you think Anya will do? What would you do?

Kicks and thrills

1 Which of these statements do you agree with? Mark them True or False.

1 Martial arts are very dangerous.
2 Karate is a very old martial art.
3 Martial arts teach self-discipline and self-confidence.
4 Judo involves hitting your opponent.

Read the pamphlet and check your answers.

Reading

2 Read the text again. Answer the questions.

1 Where were the martial arts first practised?
2 Which are the most widely-practised martial arts?
3 Does taekwondo involve hitting another person?
4 Can you find a karate club in the telephone book?
5 Why isn't it a good idea just to choose the club nearest your home?
6 Why would you be suspicious if the club didn't let you watch a class?

Martial arts

Forget bone-crunching scenes from Bruce Lee movies. The martial arts you see on the big screen look dangerous, what's taught in the gym is not. And martial arts offer good exercise, fun and mental discipline.
5 Martial arts were developed centuries ago in China, Korea and Japan. The most popular styles are taekwondo, karate and judo. Taekwondo and karate involve striking an opponent or object with hands, feet, elbows or knees. Judo requires throwing and pinning down an opponent without striking him
10 or her.

Fact file

Health benefits: You can develop power, speed, flexibility and a stronger cardiovascular system.
Other benefits: Martial arts increase self-confidence
15 and teach self-discipline, self-control and respect for others.
Equipment: At the beginning only a *gi*: a white jacket and loose trousers. Later on for karate and judo: a mouth guard. For taekwondo: the above items
20 plus gloves, padded boots, a helmet and a chest protector.

Tips on finding and choosing a class

- **Find out where you can learn.** Ask your sports teacher if he/she can recommend a place where you can learn
25 karate. You can also look in the yellow pages or contact The Sports Council.
- **Visit several clubs.** Don't simply pick the one nearest your home.
- **Find out how much it costs.** You should be able to pay
30 monthly and stop whenever you want.

- **Find out the student-teacher ratio.** It shouldn't be more than 13 to 1.
- **Find out about the teaching.** Don't be afraid of saying, 'I'd like to know how students are taught.' A good club
35 should be able to explain and invite you to watch a class. Ask what safety equipment is used.
- **Sit in on a class.** Are the students enjoying themselves? Do they show respect for one another and for the instructor?
40 - **Be sure the school instils the discipline needed to use the art responsibly.** You will be taught skills that could be used to injure others.
- **Talk to an instructor.** Instructors should have at least seven years' training experience. The answer to a direct
45 but polite 'Could you tell me why this school is better than others?' could help you make up your mind.
- **Don't be impressed by trophies.** They can be bought at sport and hobby shops.

Grammar

> **Indirect questions: a more polite way of asking questions**
>
> **1 Yes/No questions**
> Direct:
> **Do they** teach karate?
> Indirect:
> **I'd like to know if they** teach karate.
> **I was wondering if they** teach karate.
> **Can/could you tell me if they** teach karate?
>
> **2 Open (Wh-) questions**
> Direct:
> **Where can I** learn karate?
> Indirect:
> **I'd like to know where I can** learn karate.
> **Can/could you tell me where I can** learn karate?

3 Make the questions in Exercise 2 into indirect questions. Start your questions in as many different ways as you can.

EXAMPLE: 1 *Could you tell me where the martial arts were first practised?*

4 Role play. You want to learn judo and you are going to visit a club and talk to the staff.

Student A: Use the tips in the pamphlet to prepare the questions you are going to ask the staff. You will need to ask indirect questions at first but you can then ask direct questions without being impolite.

EXAMPLE: *Can you tell me how students are taught?*

Student B: You are a member of staff at the club. Answer your partner's questions.

Swap roles.

Writing

> ✸ A report is an account or description of a situation or event. It is prepared to give people information and it usually includes:
> 1 a general introduction
> 2 a description and evaluation of particular aspects of the situation/event
> 3 a conclusion or recommendation.

5 Read these extracts from a report. What part of the report do they come from, the introduction, the description/evaluation of the club's facilities, or the conclusion/recommendation?

> but the swimming pool is large and clean. The centre also has a lifeguard on duty every afternoon.

> The facilities at the Fountain Leisure Centre are on the whole adequate, but the instructors in the gym are not all qualified to teach their sport or activity. We would not recommend it for people who wish to learn martial arts.

> Our group visited the Fountain Leisure Centre. The Centre has a swimming pool, a gym and two squash courts. We talked to both staff and members in order to assess the overall quality of the centre. These are our findings:

6 Your local youth club is putting together a database of sports facilities in the area. You and your group visited a martial arts club. Based on the information from Exercise 4, write a report on the club. Follow this plan:

Introduction: (What's the name of the club? What martial arts do they teach?)

Description/evaluation of facilities: (Include information on class size, the instructors and the general conditions. Say whether you think the facilities are good or not.)

Conclusion/recommendation: (Is the club good on the whole? Would you recommend it?)

Reading

7 **Look at the photograph below and read the pamphlet. Answer these questions.**

1 What is the young man doing?
2 What is he wearing?
3 How do you think he feels?
4 What questions would you ask before jumping?
5 Find a sentence which reassures potential jumpers.
6 Find a phrase which shows that people jump from a special place.

Word watch

We can change the grammatical meaning of a word by changing the ending.
e.g. **euphoria** n *a feeling of extreme happiness and excitement*
People say post-bungee **euphoria** is quite common.
euphoric adj *a person in a state of euphoria*
Jon was so **euphoric** after the jump that he couldn't eat.
Identifying the parts of speech helps you understand a sentence and build your vocabulary at the same time.

8 **Complete the chart with words from the text.**

Noun	Adjective
. . . . . .	thrilling
exhilaration	. . . . . .
. . . . . .	euphoric
safety	. . . . . .
emotion	. . . . . .
. . . . . .	elated
enjoyment	. . . . . .
growth	. . . . . .
training	. . . . . .

Now complete the statements with *noun* or *adjective*, looking at the words in the chart.

1 '-tion', '-ty' and '-ment' are _____ endings.
2 '-able', '-ic', '-ed' and '-al' are _____ endings.

EURO B BUNGEE

The ultimate thrill

Bungee jumping is one of the world's fastest growing mass thrill sports practised by hundreds of thousands of people around the world. At Euro Bungee sites around the country, our fully trained staff will brief and guide you through this most exhilarating experience.

5

You will ascend in our purpose-built Jump Station, accompanied at all times by a trained instructor. At 60 metres with all checks complete, you will be ready to make the dive of your life . . . An experience never to be forgotten.

10

Pure adrenalin

Psychologists say it is post-bungee euphoria. Jumpers say the state of elation lasts for hours after jumping. You'll wear a broad grin on your face all day!

Safe

15 You are completely safe in our hands. All our equipment and procedures have been developed specifically for bungee jumping.

What some jumpers have said

'When I went into free fall the adrenalin rush was incredible!'
20 'It's more emotional than physical.'
'It was terrifyingly enjoyable!'
'It was one of the most fantastic feelings I've ever had.'
'I love it! It's the ultimate buzz.'

After his first jump, twenty-two-year-old Lenny Brice said it
25 was the most exciting thing he had ever done and asked when he could do it again. Twenty-three-year-old Marina Andrews said she absolutely loved the feeling of elation.
We think you'll love it too.

9 Cross out the incorrect word from the pairs in *italics*.

1 Neil said, 'Bungee jumping is the biggest *thrilling/thrill* I have ever experienced.'
2 The publicity says, 'The *safety/safe* of the equipment is guaranteed.' 'I think it looks very *safe/safety* too,' Sandra commented.
3 'Bungee jumping brings a sense of *exhilaration/ exhilarating* and *elation/elated*,' say the organisers.
4 Someone said, 'The feeling is less physical than *emotion/emotional*.'
5 'I get no *enjoyable/enjoyment* out of things like bungee jumping,' said Sandra.

Grammar

Reported speech

1 Reporting verb – present tense
a) Reporting something that is said all the time.
'The sense of elation **lasts** for hours,' jumpers **say.** ⟶ Jumpers **say** (that) the sense of elation **lasts** for hours.

b) Reporting something written.
'Bungee jumping **is** safe,' the brochure **says.** ⟶ The brochure **says** (that) bungee jumping **is** safe.

2 Reporting verb – past tense.
Reporting something said earlier.
Lenny **said**: 'It**'s** the most exciting thing I**'ve** ever **done.'** ⟶ Lenny **said** (that) it **was** the most exciting thing he **had** ever **done.**

---

10 Put the sentences in Exercise 9 in reported speech.

EXAMPLE: 1 *Neil said bungee jumping was the biggest thrill he had ever experienced.*

11 What does the bungee jumping pamphlet say about:

1 bungee jumping?
2 the popularity of bungee jumping?
3 the quality of Euro Bungee equipment?
4 their staff?
EXAMPLE: 1 *It says bungee jumping is the ultimate thrill.*

Listening

12 🖭 Listen to a potential jumper making enquiries.

a) Listen and make notes about the girl's worries.
EXAMPLE: *safe?*

b) Listen again. Make notes about the things the man says to reassure the girl.
c) Write down one way of expressing worries and three ways of reassuring people.

Get talking

13 Work in groups of three. You are all about to do a bungee jump. Things wouldn't quite look like the cartoon above!

Student A: You are not sure you want to do it. Tell B and C why you are worried.

Student B: You know A is worried. Listen to A's worries and try to reassure him/her. You must try to persuade A to jump.

Student C: You don't think it is a good idea for A to jump. You don't want to jump either. You must try to persuade him/her not to jump.

Use the expressions and ideas in Exercise 12 as well as your own. Who can persuade A?

Parents in the classroom

Reading

Efficient learners don't read word by word. They move their eyes along the lines of a text, taking in meaningful groups of about three to six words at a time.

1 Read this text silently *once*. Pause briefly at the slashes (/).

The two-hour / class / is well / under way. / Most / of the / students are / eagerly listening, / some are / actively / participating, / a few shift / uneasily / in their seats. / They are / taking / a class / on skills for / adolescence. /

Now answer these questions *without reading the text again*.

1 What subject are the students in the text studying?
2 What are the students doing? Name at least two things.

2 Read this text silently *once*. Pause briefly at the slashes (/).

The two-hour class / is well under way. / Most of the students / are eagerly listening, / some are actively participating, / a few shift uneasily / in their seats. / They are taking a class / on skills for adolescence. /

Now answer the questions in Exercise 1.

3 Answer these questions.

1 Which reading, 1 or 2, involved longer, more meaningful groups of words?
2 Which reading did not pause at the end of lines but at the end of meaningful groups of words?
3 Which questions were you able to answer better, those in Exercise 1 or those in Exercise 2? Why, do you think?

4 ▭ Read the article in an efficient way. Then listen to the questions on the cassette and write the answers after each one.

Teenagers and ho

The two-hour class is well under way. Most of the students are eagerly listening, some are actively participating,
5 a few shift uneasily in their seats. They are taking a class on skills for adolescence. Their average age is thirty-eight.
10 Thirty-eight? Surely you don't need skills for adolescence at that age? The teacher, Jane Ashby, disagrees. She's running a
15 course for parents of teenage children. She believes that caring for teenagers demands special tactics. 'For some it is an innate skill,' she says, 'but
20 others find it difficult.' She strongly suggests that those parents should go on the course.
    Angry quarrels often arise in families when differences in lifestyle come between parents and their teenage children. 'It may
25 sound silly but clothes have become a major source of tension in our family,' says one mother. 'I'd like my son to wear proper clothes when we go out. But his idea of nice clothes is a pair of jeans, an oversize T-shirt
30 and scruffy trainers!'
    Mrs Ashby recommends talking to teenagers properly, not like little children. Conflicts should be discussed in an ordered, unemotional way. Giving children clear
35 reasons for your demands could defuse a potentially explosive situation: 'Because I say so', for example, is unlikely to be accepted as a valid argument.
    Teaching parents has its difficulties.
40 Parents often have little time and energy, and teaching them requires lots of tact. The first course failed after Mrs Ashby wrote to parents suggesting that they should go on the course to 'help with problems in the
45 family'. Not wanting to admit to problems,

urvive them

nobody came. That's why she now calls the course 'Skills for adolescence'.

During the classes, she gets parents to share their own solutions to individual problems, but she also gives advice. Most parents mention problems like untidy bedrooms and late homecomings. Mrs Ashby urges them to try to reach a compromise. Agree on quite an early homecoming time during the week, but a later one at the weekend.

The student parents like the course. 'I came because being a parent is a learning process and a discussion-based class is very useful,' one mother said. One father said he only had one complaint: 'When I get home my children ask me; "And what did you learn at school today, Dad?"'

Grammar

> **Reporting advice: *advise, recommend, suggest* and *urge***
>
> Mrs Ashby: 'Why don't you talk to your teenage sons and daughters like adults?'
>
> | Mrs Ashby | **suggests** *or* **suggested** **recommends** *or* **recommended** | **(that) parents should talk** to their teenage sons and daughters like adults. **talking** to teenagers like adults. |
> | --- | --- | --- |
>
> Mrs Ashby **advises** *or* **advised talking** to teenagers like adults.
>
> | Mrs Ashby | **advises** *or* **advised urges** *or* **urged recommends** *or* **recommended** | **parents to talk** to their teenage sons and daughters like adults. |
> | --- | --- | --- |
>
> **Look!**
> *Degrees of reporting advice*
>
> *less strong* —|————|————|————|— *stronger*
> suggest   recommend   advise   urge

5 Report the advice given in these situations.

1 Mrs Bailey said to her son Alex: 'Why don't you wear something nice to your grandmother's party?'
2 Tessa told her older sister: 'If I were you, I'd come straight home after school.'
3 Paco said to his friend: 'You must talk to your parents about your problems.'
4 The headmaster tells students: 'If I were you I'd study much harder.'
5 Marian told her young brother: 'You really should show mum the teacher's note!'
6 Mrs Ashby tells parents: 'Talk more openly to your children.'

Word watch

 Some words can cause special difficulties.
Advise *and* **practise** *are verbs.* **Advice** *and* **practice** *are nouns.*

6 Cross out the incorrect word in each pair.

EXAMPLE: 1 ~~advise~~/advice

1 Course participants gave each other *advise/advice*.
2 'Keep calm and don't shout' is the best *advise/advice* I've ever had.
3 Some parents don't *practise/practice* what they preach.
4 You'll need lots of *practise/practice* to be a good parent.
5 Psychologists *advise/advice* parents to discuss rules with their teenage sons and daughters.

Listening

7 📼 **Listen to three people talking about changes in attitude since the course. Number these items 1–3.**

a) intends to start listening to what daughter says.

b) doesn't want to believe communication always helpful.

c) mum listens to son and daughter while cooking.

8 **Read the comments made by the parent and teenagers on the cassette. Fill in the blanks, using the words in the boxes.**

1 'I've got a thirteen-year-old daughter ____ chatters non-stop. When I was on the course and saw the ____ "How to stop ____ children talking", I thought, this is ____ me. Now I know it meant ____ the opposite. I think I'd better start listening ____ she stops trying to talk to me.'

before	exactly	for	topic	who	your

2 'My brother and I ____ do our homework at the ____ table while mum's making ____ . We've discussed a million things between ____ and Biology projects. It's ____ . I'd rather we had even *more* time to ____ .'

kitchen	Maths	chat	supper
sometimes	good		

3 'Since ____ parents went on the ____ , they seem to have decided it's time we talked. The ____ is, I don't ____ want to talk to them.'

my	course	always	trouble

📼 **Listen again and check your answers.**

Grammar

> **Expressing preferences and recommendations**
> **Preferences**
> Would rather
> 1 *Subject* + would rather + *infinitive*
> I **would rather talk** (= *I would **prefer** to talk*).
> *The subject of* would rather *is the same as the subject of* talk.
>
> 2 *Subject* + would rather + *subject* + *past tense*
> I **would rather we talked** (= *I would **prefer** it if we talked*).
> *The subject of* would rather *is different from the subject of* talk.
>
> **Recommendations**
> It's time
> 1 It's time + to + *infinitive*
> **It's time to talk** (= *The time has come to talk*).
>
> 2 It's time + *subject* + *past tense*
> **It's time we talked** (= *We should have talked before*).
>
> Had better + *infinitive*
> He **had better start** talking (= *He **should** start talking/It's a **good idea** for him to start talking*).

9 **Use the phrases in the box to recommend courses of action.**

EXAMPLE: 1 '*It's after 10 o'clock. You'd better go home. Your parents will be worried.*'

clean it	do your homework	go home
tell your mother	go to bed	get changed
hang up		

1 'It's after 10 o'clock. ____ Your parents will be worried.'

2 'Your room is even dirtier than mine. ____ .'

3 'You've been watching TV all evening. ____ . You don't want your teacher to get cross!'

4 'You've been on the phone for an hour. ____ Dad wants to make a call.'

5 '____ you broke the vase. She won't be so angry if you tell her you did it.'

6 'It's late and you've got school tomorrow. ____ .'

7 'Your granny will be here any minute now. ____ .'

10 Answer these questions about yourself. Use *would rather* in your answers. Give a reason for your preference in each case.

1 Your brother/sister is having a party on the same day as your best friend. Whose party would you prefer to go to?
2 You have a problem with a friend. You can talk to another friend or to your parents about it. Who would you prefer to talk to?
3 For your birthday your parents have given you a choice: either you can have a nice big present or you can have a party with all your friends. Which would you prefer them to give you?
4 You have done something wrong at school. Would you prefer your teacher to punish you by giving you extra homework or by getting you to help clean the playground?
5 Your parents will only let you go out with friends if your younger brother/sister goes along too. Would you prefer to take him/her with you or stay at home?
6 You're doing very badly at school. Would you prefer your teacher to tell your parents or would you prefer to talk to them yourself?

Writing

11 You have been asked to design a poster for one of the 'Skills for adolescence' classes. The teacher wants a poster which shows teenagers' suggestions for ways that parents and children can understand each other better.

a) Think about what to include. Decide on a style of writing (direct or indirect suggestions? Stronger or less strong recommendations? A mixture?)
b) Make the poster and show it to the class. Which is the best?

Vision of Danger

📖 EPISODE TWO

1 **What happened in Episode One? Give a brief description of Anya and say what happened to her that day.**
2 **Read Episode Two and answer these questions.**
1 How does Stefan feel about London?
2 What happens in Piccadilly Circus?
3 How do you think Stefan knows where to find the girl?
4 In what way is Stefan similar to Anya?

Stefan was excited about being in London. He had always wanted to go there. He felt that something was pulling him towards the city. At last
5 he had made it. All he had to do now was to wait for things to happen. He was sure that something would, sooner or later.

He looked out of the coach
10 window, his eyes bright with excitement. They had stopped at a traffic light in Piccadilly Circus. Suddenly, he saw her. Looking at her was almost like looking
15 at himself in a mirror. She stood on the pavement and they looked deep into each other's eyes for a brief
20 moment. Stefan's heart pounded in his chest. But just then, the coach moved forward and he lost
25 sight of her in the crowd. He had to tell the driver to stop.

'Wait!' he managed to shout.

'What is it, Stefan?' his teacher asked crossly.
30 Stefan hesitated. How could he explain that what he had waited for all his life had finally happened? 'When is our free afternoon?' he said instead.
35 'Today. Don't worry, you'll get a chance to go shopping then.'

Stefan sighed and closed his eyes, trying to lock in his mind the image of the girl. 'I *will* find her,' he said to
40 himself. 'I know I will.'

Stefan couldn't concentrate on the visit to the Crown Jewels. He was relieved when they were finally allowed to go their separate ways.
45 He decided not to join his friends for a trip on the River Thames but started instead to walk to Primrose Hill Park purposefully. He *knew* he had to go there.
50 When he got to Primrose Hill, he climbed to the top and there, sitting on a bench, was Anya.

She looked up when she heard his footsteps. 'Hello,' she said simply.
55 'I've been waiting for you.'

'I know,' he replied, approaching her. 'I'm Stefan.'

3 **Do you think Anya and Stefan will become friends?**
4 **Do you think Anya and Stefan will have any trouble communicating with each other? Why (not)?**
5 **You are Stefan and you have been in London for a few days. You have just met Anya. Write a short letter to a friend back home. Say what you have been doing and how you are feeling.**

Revision

Reading

1 Read the introductory paragraph of the article 'The elephant princess'.

a) What kind of article do you think it is going to be, serious and formal, or light and entertaining? Why?

b) What do you think the article is going to be about?

2 Read the article to check your answers to Exercise 1. Remember to read meaningful groups of words, rather than one word at a time.

The elephant princess

In India, the centuries-old relationship between man and elephant is breaking down. Each
5 species views the other with fear and suspicion. But one woman, Parbati Barua, has forged new bonds between them.

10 The elephant was lying heavily on its side, fast asleep. A few dogs started barking at it. The elephant woke up in a terrible fury: it chased the dogs into the
15 village where they ran for safety. That didn't stop the elephant. It destroyed a dozen houses and injured several people. The villagers were scared and angry.
20 Then someone suggested calling Parbati, the elephant princess.

Parbati Barua's father was a legendary hunter of tigers and leopards and an elephant tamer.
25 He taught Parbati to ride an elephant before she could even walk. He also taught her the dangerous art of the elephant round-up – how to catch wild
30 elephants.

Parbati hasn't always lived in the jungle. After a happy childhood hunting with her father, she was sent to boarding school in
35 the city. But Parbati never got used to being there and many years later she returned to her old life. 'Life in the city is too dull. Catching elephants is an adventure
40 and the exhilaration lasts for days after the chase,' she says.

But Parbati doesn't catch elephants just for fun. 'My work,' she says, 'is to rescue man from
45 the elephants, and to keep the elephants safe from man.' And this is exactly what Parbati has been doing for many years. Increasingly, the Indian elephant
50 is angry: for many years, illegal hunters have attacked it and its

home in the jungle has been reduced to small pieces of land. It is now fighting back. Whenever
55 wild elephants stray into a tea garden or a village, Parbati is called to guide the animals back to the jungle before they can kill.

Parbati is such a fragile-looking
60 woman and her voice is so soft that you would not think her capable of dealing with such huge, wild animals. Despite her appearance, she has the power to
65 make elephants obey her: she tames as well as catches elephants. Most *mahouts* (elephant tamers) can make an elephant respond to about thirty oral commands.
70 Parbati can make an elephant understand – and obey! – forty-two different commands, for example, 'Take this letter in your trunk, go to the forest and deliver
75 it to the other camp.' 'I can teach an elephant almost anything. If I found a pen big enough, I could probably teach an elephant to write,' she jokes.
80 The work of an elephant tamer also involves love and dedication. A good *mahout* will spend hours a day singing love songs to a newly captured elephant. 'Eventually they
85 grow to love their tamers and never forget them. They are also more loyal than humans,' she said, as she climbed up the trunk of one of her elephants and sat on
90 the huge, happy animal. An elephant princess indeed!

3 Read the article again. Write questions for these answers.

1 ......? It was sleeping.
2 ......? To be safe from the elephant.
3 ......? Because it had hurt some people.
4 ......? Before she could walk.
5 ......? How to catch wild elephants.
6 ......? No, she hasn't.
7 ......? She's been doing it for many years.
8 ......? Hunted it and invaded its territory.

4 What did Parbati say about these topics? Write sentences *without looking at the text*.

EXAMPLE: 1 *She said that life in the city was dull.*

1 life in the city
2 catching elephants
3 her work
4 her ability to tame elephants
5 tamed elephants
6 the loyalty of humans

5 You want to write an article about Parbati for the school newspaper.

a) Write five things you would like to know about Parbati and which 'The elephant princess' doesn't tell you.
EXAMPLE: *I'd like to know if she has ever killed a tiger.*

b) Write the questions you would ask her using your sentences in a).
EXAMPLE: *Have you ever killed a tiger?*

6 Could you have a life similar to Parbati's? Could she have a life similar to yours? Write two things that you think you and Parbati would:

1 find difficult but would get used to.
2 find impossible to get used to.
3 find easy to get used to.
EXAMPLE: *I'm not used to living with animals but I would get used to it in the end.*

Parbati is used to riding an elephant so she would never get used to driving a car.

Listening

7 💬 You are going to listen to some friends talking about Alison Hargreaves, the British climber.

a) Listen to the conversation. How do Patrick and Laura feel about these things, (un)surprised, shocked, impressed, understanding or (un)interested?
1 Patrick's article
2 the fact that Alison Hargreaves climbed Mount Everest and K2
3 the fact that the climber was a woman
4 people who put their lives in danger

b) Listen again. Write down the phrases Patrick and Laura use to express their attitude. Underline the words they emphasise.
EXAMPLE: 1 *Laura: Oh yes? (uninterested)*

c) Which things do Laura and Patrick agree/disagree on? Who do you agree with?

The wider world

8 What do you think Alison Hargreaves meant when she said it was better to have lived one day as a tiger than a thousand years as a sheep? Do you agree? Why (not)?

Project

9 In groups, you are going to write a newspaper for your town or your school.

a) Agree on what you are going to write about, for example personalities, events, etc.
b) Decide what article you each want to write. Gather your information. (Interview the people you want to write about, for example.)
c) Write your individual articles.
d) When your articles are ready, stick them on large sheets of paper to make the newspaper. Try to include some pictures if you can.

Grammar practice

1 Complete this passage with the correct form of the verbs in brackets. Use the Past Simple, the Past Continuous, the Present Perfect, the Present Perfect Continuous or the Past Perfect. (Unit 1)

Last month I *went* (1 go) to visit a bungee jumping club with my parents and my cousin. I ____ (2 not see) a jump station before so I was surprised it was so high up. My cousin ____ (3 jump) for more than a year. 'It's really the most exciting sport in the world,' she says. While my parents ____ (4 have) a cup of tea, I ____ (5 stand) at the bottom of the jump station to watch the people go up. Then one of the attendants said: 'It's your turn.' I ____ (6 realise) I ____ (7 stand) in the queue! I didn't know what to say but I really wanted to jump so I went up. Everything looked very small from the top and I was really scared. The attendant said: 'Wait a minute. ____ you ____ (8 do) this before? Can I see your card?' 'No,' I cried. 'I ____ (9 never do) it in my life. Please get me down. It's all a terrible mistake!' The attendant was very angry because I ____ (10 waste) his time but he helped me get down. It was very embarrassing. I ____ (11 tell) my parents about it but I ____ (12 have) nightmares ever since! I never want to go to a bungee jumping club again!

2 Answer the questions about the passage in Exercise 1. Use reported speech. (Unit 4)

EXAMPLE: *1 She says she was surprised it was so high up.*
1 What does the girl in the text say about the height of the jump station?
2 What does the girl's cousin say about bungee jumping?
3 What did the attendant say to the girl when she was standing at the bottom of the jump station?
4 How does the girl explain the attendant's mistake?
5 What does she say about the way things looked from the top?
6 What did she tell the attendant at the top?
7 Why does she say the attendant was angry?
8 What does the girl say about the way she has been feeling since the incident?
9 How does the girl say she feels about bungee jumping now?

3 Imagine you interview an English speaking person who has been living in your country for two months. Write a dialogue asking him/her about his/her experiences. Include the questions below. Ask mainly indirect questions at first. (Unit 4)

EXAMPLE: *I was wondering if you could answer some questions.*

• Could you answer some questions?
• How long have you been living here?
• Is this your first time in (*your country*)?
• Do you like living here?
• What do you miss the most?
• Have you made any (*your nationality*) friends?

4 Complete these sentences with *despite* or *even though* on the solid lines and *so, such,* or *such a(n)* on the dotted lines. (Units 2 and 3)

1 <u>Even though</u> the weather was nice, Simon had <u>*such a*</u> bad cold he had to stay indoors.
2 ____ the fact that there was a good film on that night, Helen was . . . tired she went to bed.
3 Erica was . . . intelligent girl that she always won prizes but ____ her intelligence she couldn't read a bus timetable!
4 ____ we trained hard our team lost the game but we are . . . determined to win next time that we are now training even harder.
5 Tom is . . . difficult child that he has been expelled from two schools. ____ his parents try hard to help him, he still gets into trouble.
6 Hungarian is . . . difficult for English people that the Browns still can't speak it well ____ they've been living in Hungary for a year.
7 The class had a video conference with a school in Argentina but ____ the modern technology the transmission was very bad. They had . . . trouble understanding each other that they gave up.

5 Rewrite these sentences using *would rather, had better* and *it's time.* (Unit 5)

EXAMPLE: *1 Mariana would rather phone than write letters.*
1 Mariana prefers phoning to writing letters.
2 My parents would prefer me not to go out so often.
3 It's very cold. You really should stay indoors.
4 You should have gone home earlier. It's late!
5 It would be a good idea to do your work now.
6 I'd prefer to learn tennis than a martial art.

6 Rewrite the sentences **A** says using *(not) be used to* or *get used to*. **(Unit 2)**

EXAMPLE: 1 *I've got stomachache because I'm not used to eating spicy food.*

1 A: I've got stomachache because I don't usually eat spicy food.
   B: Don't eat so much chilli, then.

2 A: I've got a headache because I don't usually sit in the sun.
   B: Why don't you wear a hat?

3 A: Please lend me a coat. I'm not familiar with such cold weather.
   B: And you should wear gloves too.

4 A: Reading in English was really hard for me last year but now it isn't strange any more.
   B: That's good. Now try not to use a dictionary.

5 A: I'm never late for school. I've always got up early. The trouble is I wake up early even at weekends.
   B: Keep your room dark and try to go back to sleep.

6 A: We find the food in this country less strange now but we still don't like the food at school. What do you suggest?
   B: Make your own sandwiches.

7 A: It feels strange to see my best friend with other people: we're always together. Any suggestions?
   B: Go out with other people yourself.

7 Report the advice **B** gives to **A** in Exercise 6. Use *suggest, advise* and *recommend*. **(Unit 5)**

EXAMPLE: 1 *B advised A not to eat so much chilli.*

8 What's your ideal friend like? Write six sentences about him/her using six of the adjectives in the box and the correct preposition. **(Unit 3)**

EXAMPLE: *My best friend has to be interested in football.*

interested keen afraid good embarrassed angry fond amused shocked

Grammar

1 talk about the past using a variety of tenses. (Unit 1)
2 use a variety of negative statements correctly. (Unit 1)
3 make negative questions to express surprise, disbelief, or when we expect a *yes* answer. (Unit 1)
4 talk about things people are(n't) accustomed to using *(not) be used to* and *get used to*. (Unit 2)
5 connect contrasting clauses using *even though* and *despite*. (Unit 2)
6 talk about people's emotions and interests using different adjective + preposition combinations. (Unit 3)
7 introduce a result using *so* and *such (that)*. (Unit 3)
8 make polite enquiries by using a variety of indirect questions. (Unit 4)
9 report what people say all the time, what written texts say and what was said earlier using reported speech. (Unit 4)
10 report advice using *advise, recommend, suggest* and *urge*. (Unit 5)
11 express preferences and recommendations using *would rather, had better* and *it's time*. (Unit 5)

Skills

READING

- predict the style of an article by reading the introductory paragraph. (Unit 1)
- read more efficiently by reading meaningful groups of words. (Unit 5)

WRITING

- organise and write an article. (Unit 1)
- write a report. (Unit 4)

LISTENING

- anticipate the content of a talk/interview by thinking about the sort of talk/interview you are going to hear. (Unit 1)
- identify people's attitude by listening to the words they use, the way they speak and their intonation. (Unit 3)

SPEAKING

- negotiate the solution to a problem. (Unit 2)
- express your attitude in different ways. (Unit 3)
- express concern, reassure and persuade people. (Unit 4)

29

Don't judge a book by its cover

1 **Are these statements fact, fiction or a mixture, do you think? Discuss with your partner.**

'Most young people think books make good presents. In bed is the favourite place for reading. But the bath, bathroom and toilet are popular too.'

Turn to page 102 and check your answers.

Reading

2 **Read quickly through the catalogue to find out:**

1 the titles of the longest and shortest books.
2 the titles of the books which (you think) are fictional and those which are factual.
3 the book which has the name of the publisher in its title.

3 **Read the descriptions of the books more carefully.**

a) Choose one which you would like to read. Tick (✓) the reasons for your choice. You can also add your own.

I like the title	It sounds interesting
I like the cover	It's quite short
It looks fun	I like that kind of book

b) Which one would you not like to read at all? Why not?

c) Read the descriptions of the people. Which book would make the best present for each? Why?
EXAMPLE: 1 *I would give Tomek the Bicycle Repair Manual. That way, he could keep his new bike in good condition.*

1 Tomek has just got a fantastic new mountain bike.
2 Rosalie likes reading and loves romantic novels.
3 Safiye is feeling sad so she needs something to make her laugh.
4 Max wants to impress his friends but doesn't know how.
5 Emilio likes scary books with lots of action and mystery.
6 Jo is fourteen and wants to know about other girls of her age.

WARN

Books can beco

101 Magic Tricks
Guy Frederick
Magic is fun – fun to watch, but even better fun to do yourself. 'It's
5 full of tricks you can puzzle your friends with.' (Simon, 15.) 'My friends were amazed. And so was I!' (Lisa, 14.)

Piccolo £2.50 126 pages

10 ### Bicycle Repair Manual
Richard Ballantine and Richard Grant
A handy manual that shows you how easy it is to carry out your own
15 running repairs and get maximum efficiency from your bicycle. Every job is illustrated in clear steps, using close-up photographs. 'It's the manual I'd been looking for.' (Chris,
20 16.)

Dorling Kindersley £5.99 96 pages

Goosebumps – You Can't Scare Me!
R L Stine
25 Courtney's a show off. She thinks she's really brave. She's always making Eddie and his friends look like fools.
    But now Eddie has found the
30 perfect revenge. He's going to get Courtney to Muddy Creek, where evil mud creatures are rumoured to live. Eddie doesn't believe the rumours, but they
35 might just be true . . .

Scholastic £2.99 124 pages

NG!

addictive!

Jane Eyre
Charlotte Brontë
Orphaned as a child, Jane later takes
up a position as governess to a
young girl but runs away after
discovering a horrible secret. As she
is about to get married, she receives
a telepathic message from the man
she has been in love with for a long
time. Will she go ahead with the
marriage or will she go in search of
her real love? An exciting and
intense drama.

*Penguin Popular Classics £6.99
447 pages*

The Puffin Book Of Heroic Failures
Stephen Pile
The next time your family, teachers
or friends say you're useless just tell
them the story of the Olympic
swimmer who nearly drowned; or
the boxer who was knocked out –
after ten and a half seconds,
including the ten seconds it took to
count him out! There are many,
many more hilarious true stories of
failure in this book.

Puffin £2.99 122 pages

I Was A Teenage Worrier
Ros Asquith
Letty Chubb is 15. You'll love the
book in which she describes her
hopes, her fears, her joys and her
tears. It is easily the most brilliant
and comprehensive alphabet of
teenage worry ever published.

Piccadilly £5.99 228 pages

Grammar

> **Giving important information: defining relative clauses with prepositions**
>
> **Usually (more informal): preposition towards the end of the clause**
>
> **1 People**
> Jane gets a message from a **man**. She has long been in love **with him**.
> ⟶ Jane gets a message from the man (**who/that**) she has long been in love **with**.
>
> **2 Things**
> It's full of **tricks**. You can puzzle your friends **with them**.
> ⟶ It's full of tricks (**which/that**) you can puzzle your friends **with**.
>
> **More formal register: preposition before the relative pronoun Usually written language**
>
> **1 People**
> Jane gets a message from a **man**. She has long been in love **with him**.
> ⟶ Jane gets a message from the man **with whom** she has long been in love.
>
> **2 Things**
> Jane never forgets the **institution**. She spent many years **in it**.
> ⟶ Jane never forgets the institution **in which** she spent many years.

4 Join these pairs of sentences to make one sentence. Use formal or more informal register according to the context in brackets.

EXAMPLE: 1 *She doesn't get on with the classmates (who/that) she travels to school with.*

1 She doesn't get on with some classmates. She travels to school with them. (Mandy's mum said to Mandy's teacher.)
2 Literature is one of the school subjects. Students are interested in it the most. (Written in a government report.)
3 He travels to school in one of his jackets. It got stolen. (Tom's mum said to her friend.)
4 Maths is a school subject. The majority of students have problems with it. (Written in an inspector's report.)
5 Sophie is one of my cousins. I feel most comfortable with her. (Sarah said to her husband.)
6 Few of my friends liked the book. I was very impressed by it. (Paul said to the librarian.)

Listening

You don't have to understand every word you hear when you listen to a text. Key words will probably be repeated several times: they will help you understand what the text is about. If you then want more details, listen again and concentrate on the parts you found difficult the first time.

5 ▣ **You are going to listen to the radio programme** *Book at Bedtime***.**

a) Listen. Which of the books in the catalogue is being read? How do you know?

b) Tell your partner as many details as you can remember. Try to piece together the whole extract.

c) Which parts are not totally clear to you? Tell the class.
EXAMPLE: *We didn't get the bit about a 'cordless phone'. There was something about 'punch' which we didn't understand (very well) either.*

d) Listen again. Concentrate on the parts you found difficult the first time. Check and add to your details.

6 **Work in groups. Imagine you are Eddie and his friends. You still want to frighten Courtney, but so far all your plans have failed. How do you get her to Muddy Creek or to the woods? Or do you try another plan? Agree on a plan and present it to the rest of the class. The class votes for the best plan.**

7 **Can you remember which of the books in the catalogue involves a governess, a secret and telepathy? Who is the author?**

Reading

When you read a long text or one which has a lot of information, try to concentrate on the important information first. Worry about the details later.
1 Skim the text and decide what type it is.
2 If it is a story, identify the main characters and the main elements in the plot.

8 **Skim the** *Jane Eyre* **text opposite. What kind of text is it? Where might you find it?**

published *Journey from the North* (1969), which describes her time as president of an international association of writers during World War II.

Jane Eyre, a novel by Charlotte Brontë, published
5 1847

Jane's parents have died and left her penniless. She lives with her aunt Mrs Reed and Mrs Reed's children in the north of England, which she hates. In addition Mrs Reed, who is a very unpleasant
10 character, treats Jane so badly that she becomes a difficult girl. Mrs Reed then sends her to Lowood Institution, which is a charity school for orphan girls.

Jane spends long and miserable years there
15 without love or care but she learns a great deal. She eventually becomes a teacher and is able to leave Lowood. Soon after, she finds employment as a governess and moves to Thornfield Hall, which she finds beautiful. There she teaches Mr Rochester's
20 daughter Adèle.

Adèle soon becomes very fond of Jane. Mr Rochester, who seems to be an unhappy and unfriendly man, is fascinated by Jane's intelligence and independence. They fall in love and decide to
25 get married.

On the eve of the wedding, a dark figure goes into Jane's room and tears her wedding veil. Jane is upset but tries to forget the incident. However, during the ceremony a solicitor called Briggs,
30 whom Jane has never met, announces that Mr Rochester is still married to someone else. It is then that Jane discovers the identity of the dark figure from the previous night. She is Mr Rochester's mad wife Bertha, whom he has kept shut away in the
35 attic of his enormous house.

Distressed, Jane runs away and nearly dies. She is saved by a man called St John Rivers and his sisters, who nurse her back to health. They then discover that they are long lost cousins and that
40 Jane has a fortune, which a distant uncle left her when he died. Jane is very grateful to the Rivers and agrees to marry St John.

One night, as the date of the wedding approaches, Jane hears a voice calling her. It is Mr Rochester,
45 calling her telepathically. She returns to Thornfield Hall, which mad Bertha has burnt down. Mr Rochester has been blinded and badly burnt while trying to save his wife, but she is dead. Jane and Rochester marry and in the last pages of the novel
50 we find that he partly recovers his sight.

JARRELL, Randall (1944–65) American poet and critic.

He published several volumes of poetry, his first being *Blood for a Stranger* (1942).

9 Look at the characters and places in *Jane Eyre*. Read the text again and say which person or place each of these sentences is about. There are two sentences for each one.

EXAMPLE: 1 *Mrs Reed*

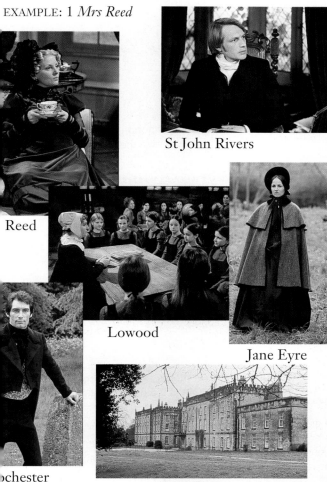

Reed

St John Rivers

Lowood

Jane Eyre

ochester

Thornfield Hall

1 She sends Jane to Lowood.
2 Jane finds it beautiful.
3 He rescues Jane.
4 She works as a governess.
5 She lives with her children in the north of England.
6 He is blinded in a fire.
7 She marries her pupil's father.
8 He is Jane's long lost cousin.
9 It is Mr Rochester's huge house.
10 It is a charity school for girls without parents.
11 It is the place where Jane lives for a long time.
12 Jane loves him.

10 Read the text again and make notes of the main elements in the plot.

EXAMPLE: *parents die, unhappy childhood*

Grammar

Giving extra information: non-defining relative clauses

These clauses are not very common in informal or spoken English.

1 People
Mrs Reed treats Jane very badly. Mrs Reed is a very unpleasant character.
        Subject of *extra information clause*
Mrs Reed, **who** is a very unpleasant character, treats Jane very badly.
Mrs Reed, **who** treats Jane very badly, is a very unpleasant character.

The writer decides which information is important and which is extra.

            Object of *extra information clause*
A solicitor called **Briggs**, **who/whom** Jane had never seen before, interrupted the ceremony.

2 Things

                Subject of *extra information clause*
Mrs Reed sends Jane to **Lowood**, **which** is a charity school for orphan girls.

                Object of *extra information clause*
Jane returns to **Thornfield Hall**, **which** Bertha has burnt down.

Look!
It is not possible to use that *in non-defining relative clauses.*

11 Use your answers to Exercise 9 to write sentences with non-defining relative clauses. When the person or place (thing) is the subject of both clauses, decide which is the important information in terms of the plot.

EXAMPLE: *Mrs Reed, who lives with her children in the north of England, sends Jane to Lowood.*

12 Work in pairs. Use your notes from Exercise 10 to write a contemporary version of the basic story in *Jane Eyre*.

Puzzling puzzles

1 How good is your knowledge of trivia? Do the quiz.

1 The giraffe has
a) the same number of bones
b) twice as many bones
c) three times as many bones
in its neck as a human being.

2 a) Henry the Eighth, King of England
b) George the First, King of England
c) Richard the Third, King of England
couldn't speak a word of English.

3 A person breathes, on average, approximately
a) 30
b) 25
c) 17
times a minute.

4 Snakes hear through their
a) eyes.
b) jaws.
c) tails.

Check your answers on page 102.

Reading

Remember that the main idea of each paragraph in a text is usually expressed in the topic sentence (often at the beginning of the paragraph). The topic sentence tells you what each paragraph is going to be about.

2 Match these topic sentences with the paragraphs in the text.

1 The test was a complete disaster.
2 It was then a matter of building the machine, which was not an easy task.
3 Sauvant was very interested in aeroplanes.
4 The next difficulty was testing the aircraft.
5 Sauvant got down to work and finally came up with a design based on his research.

Those magnificent men in their flying machines

Monsieur Sauvant was a French inventor. Although he wasn't very successful he became quite famous – as one of the world's *worst* inventors.

a ...... The Wright brothers had invented the first plane when he
5 was a child, but commercial airlines had only been operating for a few years. There had been some accidents, which worried Sauvant, so he decided to design a plane which would be completely crash-proof.

b ...... 'Aircraft should be egg-shaped,' he decided. He had been
10 doing experiments with eggs and for some time he had been observing how resistant egg shells were. Apparently he had been putting hens' eggs inside ostrich eggs and dropping them on the floor. The chicken embryo inside the hen's egg was never harmed in the fall because the larger egg protected it. How did he get the
15 hen's egg inside the ostrich egg? No one knows.

c ...... He had been working on it for a number of years – and probably spending large amounts of money – when in 1932 he was finally able to announce that he had built the perfect anti-crash aircraft. It looked like a metal egg!

20 d ...... The greatest problem was that nobody thought it would work. On three occasions the police removed the wheels from the strange-looking machine to prevent him taking off. Monsieur Sauvant was not discouraged and asked some friends to help him test the machine. At first they were not willing to help, but Monsieur
25 Sauvant seemed so sure of himself that in the end they agreed. They pushed him off a 25 metre cliff in the South of France.

e ...... When his friends looked down onto the beach, they were horrified. They had been expecting to see Monsieur Sauvant get out and wave. Instead, they saw that the machine had been totally
30 wrecked. Luckily Monsieur Sauvant was not badly hurt.

Later, when he had recovered, he declared that he was delighted with the success of the experiment!

Another magnificent man in his flying machine!

3 Answer these questions about the text.

1 What was the basis of Sauvant's invention?
2 Why wouldn't the police let him test his machine?
3 How did he eventually test it?
4 Why was the test a disaster?
5 What do you think about Monsieur Sauvant?

Grammar

Past Perfect Continuous
had + been + *verb*-ing

1 *To emphasise the **duration** of an action going on continuously before a point in the past.*

1928   1929   1930   1931   1932

— Now

He was working on his aircraft.   He announced his machine was ready.

He'd/had been working on his aircraft **for** several years when he finally announced that the machine was ready.

2 *To emphasise the **repetition** of an action before a time in the past.*

— Now

He put several hens' eggs in ostrich eggs.   He decided the aircraft should be egg-shaped.

He'd/had been putting hens' eggs inside ostrich eggs before he decided that the aircraft should be egg-shaped.

---

4 Complete the sentences by using the Past Simple or the Past Perfect Continuous form of the verbs in brackets.

1 When Leonardo da Vinci built his helicopter he _____ (work) on his design for many years. He _____ (draw) birds in flight to learn about aerodynamics.
2 We _____ (fly) for twenty minutes when the pilot _____ (announce) we had to go back because of bad weather.
3 The teacher _____ (ask) for my project on inventions for weeks when I finally _____ (give) it to her last Monday.
4 I found out why my pen friend _____ (not get) my letters. I _____ (send) them to the wrong address!
5 Our favourite band _____ (play) for only ten minutes when there _____ (be) a power cut and the concert had to be cancelled. We were upset because we _____ (die) to see them for years.

5 You are a magazine reporter in the 1930s. You interview Monsieur Sauvant after the crash, while he is recovering in hospital. Your readers want to know all about Monsieur Sauvant and his invention and his plans for the future. Write up your interview in the form of the original dialogue.

EXAMPLE:

Q *Why did you first decide to design a crash-proof plane?*

A *As you know, at that time there were already planes in operation. But the makers had been having problems with them. There had been a few accidents . . .*

Word watch

When you want to give more specific information about something or someone you can put one noun in front of another noun. You do this to specify:
• *what something is made of: a* **glass ball** *(a ball made of glass)*
• *what someone does: a* **tennis player** *(someone who plays tennis)*
• *where something is found:* the **kitchen table** *(the table in the kitchen)*
When two nouns are used together so often that they become a fixed expression, they are called **compound nouns***. e.g. a bookseller.*

6 What do you call:

1 someone who teaches English?
2 a jacket made of leather?
3 ice cream made of chocolate?
4 someone who trains dogs?
5 the window in your bedroom?
6 the library in your school?
7 the laces on your shoes? (one word)
8 the driver of a taxi?
9 a shirt made of cotton?

EXAMPLE: 1 *an English teacher*

7 Try this puzzle. Look at the pictures and with a partner try to work out what they are of.

EXAMPLE: 1
BASIA: *That looks like hair.*
ELA: *Yes, but I don't think it's human hair.*

1
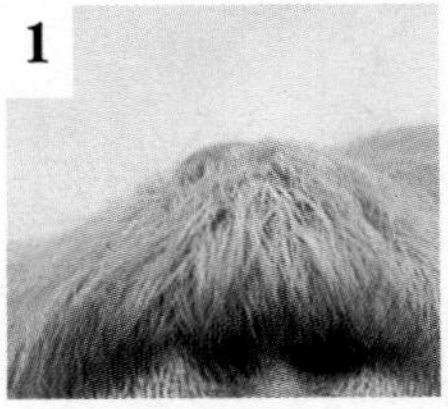

2
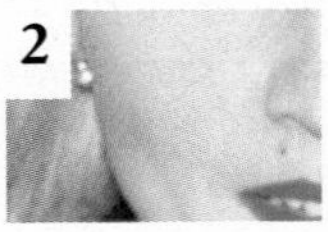

3
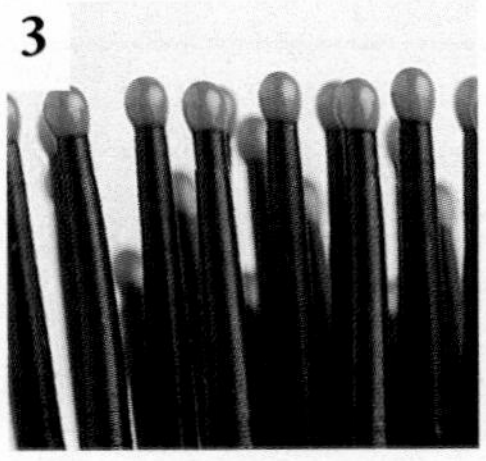

4
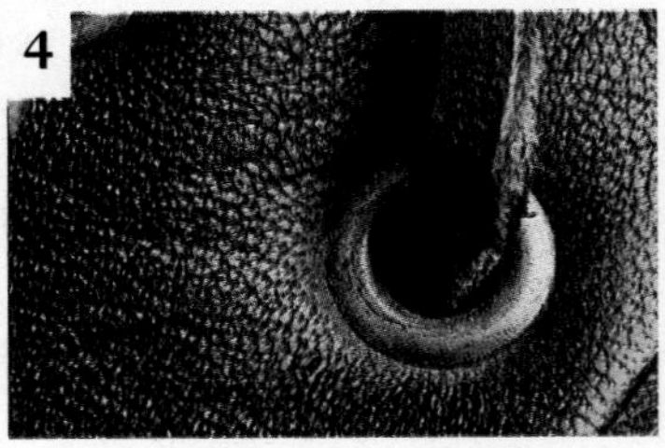

Listening

8 Listen to Jamie and Sarah solving the puzzle.

a) Were you right?
b) Listen again and answer the questions.
1 Where are Jamie and Sarah?
2 Does Sarah like doing puzzles in the car? Why (not)?
3 What does Jamie think when Sarah says she gets car sick?
4 Who is better at solving puzzles?
5 Why does Jamie say he feels sick, do you think?

Grammar

Possessives

1 **Talking about things which belong to people and animals: noun + *'s***
noun (the owner) + 's + *noun (the possession)*
It can't be a **lion's mane.** *(the mane belongs to a lion)*
It's part of **Madonna's face.** *(the face belongs to Madonna)*

2 **Talking about things which belong to other things or which are part of other things: *the . . . of***
noun (the part) + of + *article* + *noun (the whole)*
Can you read the **title of the book?**
The **bristles of a hairbrush.**

3 **Talking about one of several 'possessions' of a person (double genitive)**
a + *noun (the 'possession')* + of + *noun* + *'s/possessive pronoun*
He is **a friend of Sarah's.** = *one of Sarah's friends*
Tim is **a cousin of hers.** = *one of her cousins*

Look!
I went to my friends**'** house.✓
I went to my friends's house.✗ *(plural noun ending in* s*)*

That is Charles's car.✓
(name or singular noun ending in s*)*

John and Molly**'s** house✓
John's and Molly's house ✗ *('s after the last name only)*

9 Rewrite the sentences using the correct possessive form of the nouns in brackets.

EXAMPLE: 1 *I was bored so I borrowed my brother's puzzle book.*

1 I was bored so I borrowed (puzzle book/my brother).
2 We drove for hours in (car/my father).
3 I enjoy reading (letters/my pen friend).
4 You can find the solution to the puzzle in the (back/book).
5 The (house/windows) are all broken.
6 (hair/my friend) looks like a (mane/lion).
7 Let's sit at the (bus/front).
8 I always have fun when I go to (house/my cousins). They really know how to enjoy themselves.
9 (cat/Mr and Mrs Jones) always comes into my room.

10 Rewrite the sentences so that they mean the same.

EXAMPLE: 1 *Bina is a friend of mine.*

1 Bina is one of my friends.
Bina is . . .
2 One of her uncles plays in a band.
An . . .
3 One of my mother's friends has invented a new game.
A friend . . .
4 Laurie always taps her foot on the floor when she's bored. It's one of her little habits.
Tapping her foot on the floor . . .
5 One of our cousins is moving to another country.
A . . .
6 He is wearing one of his father's old suits to the party. He says it's fashionable!
He is wearing an . . .

11 Look at these photographs. Match the features with the people.

Sylvester Stallone Nicole Kidman Kevin Costner
Arnold Schwarzenegger Cindy Crawford

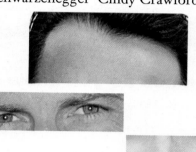

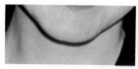

1 **How did Anya and Stefan meet? Where are they now?**
2 **Read Episode Three and answer these questions.**
1 How many brothers and sisters has Anya got?
2 What exactly do Anya and Stefan have in common?
3 What do Stefan and Anya hear in the park?
4 How do you think Anya knew she would meet someone like Stefan?

Anya and Stefan stood at the top of the hill, smiling at each other. The whole of London lay at their feet.
5 Stefan spoke first. 'How long have you known?' he asked.
Anya smiled. 'That we would meet? All my life, I think. Of course I didn't know it would be you in
10 particular. But I've always known that there was someone, somewhere, just like me.'
'I know what you mean,' Stefan said. 'Hey, let's play a game! I'll tell
15 you what I think you're like and you tell me if I'm right, OK? Mmm. You're seventeen. You're an only child. You have few friends because people think you're strange, just like me
20 and – ' Stefan stopped. Anya had been nodding to everything he said but then she suddenly went pale.
'Anya, what is it?'

Vision of Danger

🔲 EPISODE THREE

'I don't know. I've got butterflies
25 in my stomach again,' she said.
'You're probably tired. It's been an exciting day and – '
'Shh! Can you hear that?' Anya said.
30 'What? I can't hear anything!'
'No. You're right. I'm probably imagining things.'
They walked across the deserted park, swapping information about
35 their lives and finding out all the things they had in common. Suddenly Stefan said: 'Wait, I can hear it now. It's a song, isn't it?'
'Yes. It sounds like Stone, my
40 favourite singer. Someone must be listening to a radio somewhere,' Anya said.

'He's my favourite too, but I've never heard this song before. It's a
45 bit weird, isn't it? Can you make out the words?'
Anya recited them:
Orpheus, Orpheus, beware!
There is danger in the air.
50 *Your songs and voice are sweet*
But the dragon has come to eat.
'What does it mean?' asked Stefan, frowning.
'I don't know. But whatever it is, I
55 don't like it.'

3 **Stefan and Anya have quite a lot in common. Make a list of things that you and your closest friend have in common.**
4 **How is Anya feeling at the end of this episode? Why? What do you think the words of the song might mean? What could the danger be?**

Home and away

1 Do the quiz.

How much do you know about _____ ?

Match the words with the definitions.

1 the process of making the air, water or soil dirty or dangerous

2 in danger of disappearing from the world

3 a person who specialises in the study of plants

4 animals and plants living in natural conditions

5 natural surroundings, especially in beautiful and open country

6 protection from damage or destruction

7 a wet tropical forest with tall trees growing close together

s<u>c</u>enery

<u>c</u>onservation

<u>p</u>ollution

wi<u>l</u>dlife

rain for<u>e</u>st

enda<u>n</u>gered

b<u>o</u>tanist

Now take the underlined letter in each word. Put the letters in the right order to make a word to complete the title.
To check your answer, turn to page 102.

2 Complete the sentences with words from the quiz.

1 Traffic causes *pollution*.
2 People can help save _____ animals.
3 My father is a _____. He has taught me to respect nature.
4 Last year we had a weekend at a _____ camp. We went on a nature trail and we planted some trees.
5 I read an article in the paper about the _____ in South America. Every year, thousands of trees are cut down to make paper and furniture.

Word watch

*English nouns can be **countable** or **uncountable**.*
*Countable nouns can be counted. You can use **a** or **an** with the singular form and they have a plural form:*
a bird – two birds   a plant – ten plants
Singular countable nouns cannot be used alone:
The tree is beautiful. ✓ ~~Tree is beautiful~~. ✗
*Uncountable nouns cannot be counted. You cannot normally use **a** or **an** before them and they have no plural form:*
~~a wildlife~~ ✗ ~~wildlives~~ ✗ (some) wildlife ✓
Uncountable nouns can be used alone:
The pollution is dreadful today. ✓ Pollution is awful. ✓

3 Practise what you have just revised about English nouns.

a) Underline the nouns in the sentences in Exercise 2.
b) Are they countable singular, countable plural or uncountable?
c) Look at your lists. Which noun can be both countable and uncountable?

Reading

4 Read the brochure opposite and add more nouns to the lists in Exercise 3.

5 Complete the fact file on the International Conservation Scouts. Under 'Comments', include your opinion – both positive and negative thoughts – of the scheme.

FACT FILE

Name:
International Conservation

Scouts

Locations: ....

Number of camps: ....

Aim: ....

Trained leaders?
Yes ☐   No ☐

Experience necessary?
Yes ☐   No ☐

Activities: ....

Prices from: ....

Comments: ....

....

You can make the difference between this . . . and this.

How?

This summer, join the International Conservation Scouts on a fun-filled holiday with a difference. Year after year, young people from all around the world get together at one of our sixteen conservation camps. Their shared aim? To help protect the countryside and its wildlife.

5 Many animals and plants are in danger of disappearing forever. The dormouse, for example, needs woodland plants for food and trees to nest in. Its habitat is being destroyed by man and it needs our help to survive.

10 On a conservation camp holiday you will learn all about nature and how to protect it. Our trained leaders will accompany you and tell you everything you need to know. Because of this you don't need any experience, just energy and enthusiasm. You 15 will explore the countryside and work to ensure the survival of hundreds of animals and plants and still have plenty of time to enjoy the camp's excellent sports facilities and organised nature trails through beautiful scenery.

20 The International Conservation Scouts is a worldwide organisation, so there is bound to be a camp near you. You can spend a fabulous holiday at any of the camps for as little as £60 including accommodation and food.

25 For more information send for a free conservation camps brochure today.

International Conservation Scouts
Stanton St John
Oxfordshire OX7 1TL

30 THE KEY TO SAVING WILDLIFE IS TO PROTECT NATURAL HABITATS: *YOUR* WORK WILL MAKE A DIFFERENCE.

Grammar

---

a, an, or the?

1 **Making general statements**
zero article + plural noun/uncountable noun
Dormice are European woodland animals.
All of them

Sometimes: a/an *or* the *+ singular noun*
A/The dormouse is a European woodland animal.
Talking about the class in general

2 **Referring to any one of several**
a/an *+ singular noun*
There is bound to be **a camp** near you.

3 **Talking about something unique**
the *+ name/noun*
Join **the International Conservation Scouts.**

4 **Mentioning something for the first time**
a/an *+ singular noun*
Talking about something already mentioned or known to the listener/reader
the *+ singular noun*
She went to **a conservation camp** in Scotland. At **the camp** she learnt all about nature.

For other uses of a/an *look at the grammar information on page 107.*

---

6 **Choose the correct alternative in the brackets.**

1 (An environmentalist/Environmentalist) is (person/a person) who tries to prevent the destruction of (a natural world/the natural world).

2 I'm surprised you haven't heard about the protests! There are plans to build (a new road/the new road). (The conservationists/ Conservationists) all over the country are protesting about the plans for (a road/the road) because it could destroy wildlife in the area.

3 I'd like to visit (an ecological park/ecological park). I've never been to one.

4 (Dodos/The dodos) were large birds in the pigeon family. (The dodo/Dodo) became extinct many years ago because it was hunted by hungry sailors.

7 **Complete the sentences using *a*, *an*, or *the* where necessary.**

1 ____ African rhinos are killed for their horns. That is why ____ World Wide Fund for Nature is trying to protect them.

2 A lot of people think it's bad to keep ____ wild animals in ____ cages.

3 There are two new chimpanzees in ____ city zoo: ____ male and ____ female. ____ female is smaller than ____ male.

4 There is ____ fox in the park near my house. My neighbour doesn't let her cat out at night because she's afraid ____ fox will eat it!

8 **Read this letter carefully. Complete the information in the box opposite.**

Ul. Nowy Świat 24
00-946 Warsaw

26th March 1996

International Conservation
Scouts
Stanton St John
Oxfordshire OX7 1TL

Dear Sir/Madam,

I am writing to ask for more information about your conservation camps. I read your brochure and found the idea of conservation holidays very appealing.

I am a fifteen-year-old Polish student and I am learning English at school, so I would like to go to a camp in Great Britain. Could you please tell me if there is one in Scotland? I would also like to know what the price is for two weeks in July.

I wonder if you could send me brochures of the other camps in Great Britain, too. Some friends of mine are also interested in going on a conservation holiday.

I look forward to hearing from you.

Yours faithfully,

Basia Kowalska

Basia Kowalska (Miss)

Formal letter: asking for information

Greetings:
a) You know the person's name: *Dear Mr/Mrs/Ms/Miss Sinclair* ⟶ *Yours sincerely,*
b) You don't know the person's name: . . . . . .

Addresses:
a) Write sender's address in the . . . . . . corner
b) Write other person's address . . . . . .

Useful closing sentence when expecting a reply . . . . . .

Useful expressions to ask for information:
a) *Could you please tell me if . . .*
b) . . . . . .
c) . . . . . .

9 You want to go on a conservation holiday.

a) Look at the fact file in Exercise 5 and make a note of three things you would like to know.
EXAMPLE: *what sport possible?*

b) Write a letter to the International Conservation Scouts asking for the information you want. Look at the box above for help.

10 Find out these things about your partner.

1 How he/she feels about travelling, especially to other countries.
2 What he/she is mostly interested in doing on a trip abroad.
3 How he/she feels about trying new food.

Listening

When you listen to a conversation in English, ask yourself:
1 What are the speakers talking about in general?
2 What are they specifically talking about?
3 What do the speakers think about the topic?

11 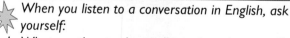 **Listen to this conversation.**

a) What is the general topic?
b) Listen again. Which specific aspects are mentioned?
• education • food • houses • customs
• clothes • the advantages/disadvantages of foreign exchanges
c) Which speaker would like to go on a foreign exchange? Which one wouldn't? Why (not)?

Grammar

The or zero article?

1 Plural/uncountable nouns
a) *referring to a class of things/ people in general*
Chopsticks are used a lot in Japan.
b) *referring to something in particular*
The rice in Japan is tasty.

2 Nationality nouns: referring to the people in general
a) *ending in* sh, ch, ss *or* ese
The Japanese eat more rice than bread.
b) *all others except* **the** Scot**s**
(The) Brazilian**s** are friendly.

12 Fill in the blanks with *the* where necessary.

1 ____ food in Britain is different from ____ food in Japan. ____ Japanese tend to eat a lot more fish than ____ British.
2 ____ Chinese have an interesting way of eating ____ eggs: they keep them in ____ mud and ____ straw for months. They are best eaten when they are a year old.
3 ____ foreign exchanges are a good way to break down ____ young people's prejudices about other cultures. ____ young people we met the other day were from Brazil.

Pronunciation

13 How is the word *the* pronounced?

a) ⌨ Listen and write down the sentences.
b) Listen again. Is *the* pronounced:
   1 / ðə / or 2 / ðɪ/?
c) Complete the rule from your answers to b):
   the + consonant sound = / /
   the + vowel sound = / /

14 Have you ever been abroad or to a different area in your country? How different was it from home? Make notes under these headings.

• Place
• Different things I ate
• Things that surprised me

Present your information to the rest of the class.

Myths and legends

1 **Look at the volumes of the encyclopedia. Write the number of the volume where you would find information about:**

- myths and legends
- the British Isles
- the phases of the moon
- your country
- Zulus
- the sea
- the solar system

Reading

⭐ *When you read a text to find* **specific information** *(for example, when you are looking up information in an encyclopedia) don't read all of the text.*

1 Scan the text: run your eyes over it and stop only at the places where you think the information is. Read those sections more carefully.

2 If the information isn't clear to you, look for examples and pictures.

2 **Scan the encyclopedia page to find a definition of *legend* and of *myth*. Remember to read on if you don't understand the definition.**

3 **What is the difference between a myth and a legend? Explain the difference to your partner in your own words. Does he/she agree with your explanation?**

Myths and legends

Myths are traditional stories occurring in a timeless past. They involve supernatural elements and are beyond the frontiers of logic. Long ago, when our ancestors heard
5 the sound of thunder and saw lightning, they were often frightened because they could not understand why these things happened. In order to understand these and other natural events, they created stories.
10 The stories were handed down from generation to generation all around the world.

Although myths are not based on objective truth, they reflect both universal worries
15 and the worries of specific cultures. The presence of the sun in the sky was a mystery in different parts of the world. In the cold northern countries, where the sun disappears almost completely during the
20 winter, great fires were lit in midwinter to help the sun to be reborn.

The ancient Greeks tell a myth in which Prometheus stole fire from Zeus, the chief god, and gave it to humans so that they
25 could keep themselves warm. To punish him, Zeus chained Prometheus to a rock where his liver was eaten by an eagle every day but grew again every night.

Legends, however, are stories about real
30 people who are famous for doing something brave or extraordinary. Every time the story was told, it became more exaggerated and so it is now difficult to tell how much of the story is really true.

35 One of the greatest legendary figures in Britain is King Arthur. He was the son of King Uther Pendragon, a Celtic King. King Uther gave his child to Merlin the wizard. Merlin taught Arthur everything he knew
40 so that he could become a great king. When King Uther died, Merlin stuck a sword into a rock and said, 'This sword is in the stone by magic. Only the true king will be able to pull it out.' Many men tried but none
45 succeeded. When Arthur tried, the sword slipped out easily. Arthur was made king. He went on to found the Round Table, an order of knights who became famous for fighting the wicked and helping the poor.

50 Some names of the **Thunder god** around the world: **Thor** (northern Europe), **Kami-nari** (Japan), **Zeus** (Greece), **Shiva** (India), **Jupiter** (Rome) , **Viracocha** (South America)

See also:
Creation myths,
55 Egyptian myths, Fire,
Northern European
myths, Robin Hood,
Seasons, Sun

4 You are reading the encyclopedia page when your little sister comes and says she needs the answer to these questions. Where in the encyclopedia do you tell her to look for the answers?

1 What was the Egyptian Sphinx?
2 Why do we have spring, summer, autumn and winter?
3 Who was Thor?
4 What happens when you light a match?

5 Read the text again and match the columns.

Action	Purpose
1 Myths were created	a) in order to punish him.
2 People in northern countries would light a fire in the middle of winter	b) so that he could be a good and wise king.
3 Prometheus stole fire from Zeus	c) so that the true king would be revealed.
4 Zeus attached Prometheus to a rock	d) so that the sun could be born again.
5 Merlin taught Arthur all he knew	e) in order to explain natural occurrences people couldn't understand.
6 Merlin stuck the sword in the stone	f) so that humans could keep warm.

Grammar

Expressing purpose

1 Same subject for both clauses
(in order) to + *verb*

Action		Purpose
People created myths	**(in order) to**	explain natural events they couldn't understand.
People lit big fires	**in order so as** **not to**	lose the sun forever.

Subject: **people**

2 Same or different subject for each clause
so (that) + *subject* + will/would *or* can/could + *verb*

Action		Purpose
Prometheus **stole** fire from Zeus	**so (that)**	humans **could** keep themselves warm.
Parents **tell** their children stories at bedtime		the children **can** go to sleep easily.
People **created** myths		they **wouldn't** be afraid of nature.

6 Read the pairs of sentences. Which is the action? Mark it A. Which is the purpose of the action? Mark it P.

EXAMPLE: 1 *The teacher gave us a text.* A *We could learn about legends.* P

1 The teacher gave us a text. We could learn about legends.
2 Find some information for my project. I looked in the encyclopedia.
3 My sister could do her homework well. I helped my sister.
4 I keep a vocabulary book. Learn new words.
5 I studied hard last year. Pass my exams.
6 Kerry bought a new camera. Take photos on her holiday.
7 Alex came in very quietly. Not to wake up his parents.

7 Write sentences using the pairs in Exercise 6. Use *to, in order to* or *so (that)*.

EXAMPLE: 1 *The teacher gave us a text so (that) we could learn about legends.*

8 Look at your sentences in Exercise 7. Rewrite the sentences with *(in order) to* using *so (that)*.

EXAMPLE: 2 *I looked in the encyclopedia so (that) I could find some information for my project.*

9 Make sentences about legendary and mythical figures using the information below. Can you and your partner add more myths?

Legend/myth	Action	Purpose
1 Robin Hood	steal from the rich	help the poor
2 The Norse gods	eat golden apples	stay young forever
3 Thor, the storm god,	use lightning	giants not hurt the gods
4 Odysseus	blind the Cyclops	he and his men escape
5 Orpheus	sing to Hades, the king of the underworld,	his dead wife, Eurydice, come back to life

Get talking

10 In pairs, work out the story of Old Man Winter and Summer Queen, an Amerindian myth.

a) Read the beginning and end of the myth.

North American Indians told this story to explain why it is cold in winter and warm in summer . . .

. . . So, for six months every year, Summer Queen stays in the south, and Old Man Winter rules the north. Then Summer Queen forces him back to his snow kingdom in the far north and brings back spring.

b) To work out the main part of the story:
Student A: Turn to page 105.
Student B: Turn to page 106.

11 Look at the pictures and read the clues. Who were these famous people?

1 Nobody got to eat the apple, but his son was OK.
2 His shows were explosive and became legendary.
3 She prevented others from dying in the colony but never got back alive herself.

If you don't know, look at the answers on page 104.

Reading

12 Look quickly at the text opposite. What kind of text is it?

13 Read the text more carefully. Match the topics with the correct paragraphs (2–6).

- An entertaining couple
- Fame and recognition
- The start of a brilliant career!
- The legend lives on
- Tragedy strikes

14 Draw a simple sketch illustrating one of Annie Oakley's shooting tricks mentioned in the text. Show it to your partner and explain what is happening in your picture.

Grammar

Too and enough

1 **too** + *adjective* (+ *to* + *infinitive*)
Annie was very young . . .
She was **too young to hold** a gun properly. Her hands were **too small**.
Her little hands just couldn't do it.

2 **(not +) *adjective* + enough (+ to + *infinitive*)**
Her father thought she was **not strong enough to hold** a gun.
She proved not only that she was **strong enough**, but that she could do it very well.
He thought she did not have the physical power to do it. She showed everybody that she had the strength, and the ability.

OAKLEY, Annie

Born 1860 in Darke County, Ohio, USA. Sharp-shooting star of the Wild West. Died 1926, aged 66.

Phoebe Anne Moses was born on a
5 farm. When she was very young, she used to watch her father and his friends shoot animals: she wanted to try too. They laughed at her because they thought she was too young and not
10 strong enough to hold a gun properly.

But she surprised them all by learning to shoot and becoming very good at it. Her family were quite poor, too poor to give Annie a good education. When she
15 was a child, her family had to borrow money from the bank to keep their farm. Annie hunted game, which she sold to help pay the mortgage on the family farm: no rabbit was quick
20 enough to escape her bullets!

Annie married a marksman whom she met at a shooting competition. Together they started their own shooting show and they performed in
25 variety shows and circuses around the country.

When Annie Oakley (her stage name) was twenty-five, the legendary Buffalo Bill saw her perform and said
30 she was too good to perform in small shows: her skills deserved a bigger, better-known show. That year, she and her husband joined the famous 'Buffalo Bill's Wild West Show'. For the
35 seventeen years that she was part of the show, Annie was the main attraction.

She was such a good shot that she could split a playing card from the side, standing ten metres away. She could hit
40 a coin thrown in the air and even shoot cigarettes held between her husband's lips. Annie Oakley travelled to Europe with the Wild West Show. When she was in Berlin, the Kaiser Wilhelm
45 insisted that she shoot a cigarette from his lips.

When Annie was forty-one, she was seriously injured in a train crash. Everyone thought that would be the end
50 of her career. But she recovered quickly and as soon as she was well enough to perform she continued to amaze her audiences for many years.

In 1946, years after her death, a
55 musical called *Annie Get Your Gun* was written about Annie Oakley. However, she was much quieter in real life than the character in the musical. Some of the stories about her shooting skills are
60 almost too extraordinary to be true. Annie Oakley has become a legendary figure of the Wild West.

15 Read the situations and fill in the blanks using *too, enough* or *not enough* and the correct form of the words in brackets.

EXAMPLE: 1.1 *isn't old enough to drive*

In Britain, people cannot drive until they are seventeen. At sixteen, Marcia ____ (1 be old/drive). Peter is a lot more irresponsible than Marcia, but, being seventeen, he ____ (2 be old/drive). Mrs Maple has sold her car. She's now eighty-five and she feels she ____ (3 be old/drive).

It was a disastrous day for the school football team. Peter had got measles and, although he was better, he ____ (1 be well/play). John had a bad case of food poisoning and ____ (2 be ill/play).

These days, you have to be 1.70m or more to be a model. At 1.50m Susan ____ (1 be short). Nadia, quite tall at 1.68m ____ (2 be tall). Rachel (1.73m) ____ (3 be tall), but she isn't interested in modelling.

16 What things is it possible or not possible for you to do at your age in your country?

EXAMPLE:

JUAN DIEGO: *I'm sixteen and I live in Mexico, so I'm old enough to drive.*

Writing

> When you write a biography, it is a good idea to:
> • have as an introductory paragraph the person's date and place of birth (and when he/she died) as well as a sentence or two about his/her achievements.
> • make notes about the most important events in the person's life. Include events from different stages of his/her life.
> • write a paragraph or two about each stage of the person's life.

17 Write a biography of your favourite legendary figure.

a) Write an introductory paragraph and make notes about the most important events in the person's life.

b) Complete the plan with your notes.
   Paragraph 1: Early life:
   Paragraph 2: Adult life and main achievements:
   Paragraph 3: Conclusion and rounding off:

c) Use your plan to write a biography.

Rocking 'n' rolling

1 Have you ever been to a pop concert or seen one on television? Tick (✓) the things the concert had. Which are essential for a good pop concert in your opinion?

- videos
- good sound equipment
- a large crowd
- programmes and other merchandise

- a light show
- a good atmosphere
- several bands
- great music!

Reading

2 Read the article. Which of the things in Exercise 1 did U2's Zooropa show include? Do you think it was a good show? Why (not)?

U2's Zooropa show: the ultimate audio-visual experience

The day before the concert Wembley Stadium looked . . . well . . . like a
5 football stadium. But the transformation was about to begin. The list of things to do was enormous:
10 miles of electronic cable needed connecting, the stage needed building and the £2 million sound equipment
15 needed unpacking and setting up. It seemed an impossible job, but U2's road crew can set up all 1,200 tonnes of
20 equipment – including the giant video screens, or vidiwalls, at the sides of the stage – in 24 hours.

25 U2's essential electronic equipment: a celebration of technology.

30 **The video 'confessional'** is in the middle of the stadium. 'From the moment the doors open, the fans can go in,'
35 says Peter Williams, one of the designers of the show. 'They can then talk to camera for thirty seconds about things
40 which are important to them. The best bits are selected and then we need to edit them before the show. They
45 are played during the show that night.'

The video studio is built under the stage. From here, the video
50 crew operate ten video laser-disc players in order to get exciting visual effects. Before the show, ten hours of video
55 material need to be put together. The video crew film the band before they go on stage. Then the seventeen-strong crew
60 directed by Maurice Linnane and Ned O'Hanlon mix in video footage from the video of the band, the video
65 confessional and satellite TV. The laser discs need to be loaded so that they play at the right time and in
70 sequence. Zooropa does not include the usual coloured lights of other rock concerts – Williams considers them old-
75 fashioned – but video is an integral part of the show.

The mixer. Apart from the visuals, it is
80 the music that attracts the audiences. The key tool is the mixer or mixing desk. Cables take the sound from
85 microphones and instruments to a mixing desk set among the audience. Here, sound engineer Joe
90 O'Herlihy and his assistants need to adjust the volume of each instrument and each voice for a perfect
95 balance of sound. Also brought to the mixer is the sound from the band's own satellite receiver, a telephone line
100 on which you can phone anywhere in the world directly. Bono, the lead singer, phones regularly during the show. On the
105 American tour, he phoned The White House and later tried to order 10,000 pizzas from a restaurant!

3 Label the diagram of **Wembley Stadium** with words from the text.

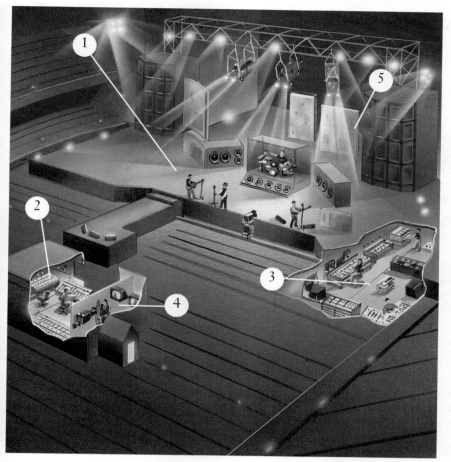

Write a short caption for each item in your own words.

Grammar

Talking about things which are necessary or very important

Need

1 The agent is known.

subject + need + to + *infinitive* + *object*
(person who   *(thing which*
does   *requires action)*
action)

Joe O'Herlihy **needs to adjust** the volume.
It is necessary for Joe – a sound engineer – to adjust the volume.

2 The agent is not known or not important.

subject + need + *verb*-ing / to be + *verb (Past Participle)*
(thing which
requires action)

The sound equipment **needs unpacking/to be unpacked.**
It doesn't matter who does it, but somebody must do it.

4 Rewrite the sentences using *need to, need -ing* or *need to be....*

EXAMPLE: 1 *You need to buy the tickets in advance.*

1 It is very important for you to buy the tickets for the concert in advance.
2 The CD player is broken. Someone must mend it.
3 It is essential to test the microphones before the concert.
4 You have to fix the lights before the disco.
5 Is it absolutely necessary for you to buy a programme?
6 It is very important to check the fire doors before the concert.
7 It is important for you to check your answers when you finish the exercise.
8 Someone must check everyone's tickets at the gate.

5 What things do the road, video and sound crews need to do *before* and *during* the concert? Read the text and write as many sentences as you can in three minutes.

EXAMPLE: *Before – The road crew need to build the video studio.*

6 Role play

Student A: You are a member of U2's crew. Choose where you want to work: the video studio or the mixing desk. Read the relevant part of the text again and use it and your own ideas to make a mental picture of your job.

Student B: You are a journalist for *Rolling Stone* magazine. Introduce yourself and interview a member of U2's crew about his/her job.

Swap roles: Student B is a member of the crew. Student A is the journalist.

Reading

7 Look at the picture with the newspaper article.

1 What idea does it convey to you?
2 Look at the title too. What do you think the article is going to be about?

Read the article to check your answer to question 2.

Rocking all over the world from a room in North London

A British band's world 'tour' by telephone could mean the end of live concerts as we know them.

5 Future Sound of London is the first group in the world to play all its 'live' shows down the telephone. They have 'toured'
10 Europe and America without leaving their studio in London and only talk to their fans through the Internet global computer network.

15 Last month, the electronic duo performed to 500 people in New York while still in their old studio in London. The audience watched complex, three-dimensional
20 images sent via the Internet. The music they heard was as clear as if it had been live. It was played in London and converted into digital pulses at the band's mixing
25 desk. The pulses were carried across the Atlantic by a digital telephone line. As soon as the computer workstations were switched on in The Kitchen
30 art gallery the pulses were re-converted into sounds.

Future Sound of London – Brian Dougans and Gary Cobain – have a team of people who look
35 after the technical side of things. Film, computer graphics and animation are being put together to create perfect sound and 3D visuals so audiences around the
40 world will be able to go to virtual reality concerts. They can then take part by using computer workstations.

Will this new technology bring
45 about an entertainment revolution? 'Jumping around on stage is old hat and on its way out,' says Dougans. His partner agrees. 'Right here in this room we're
50 doing everything: we're doing art, television, music, games, CD-ROMs, and they're all coming together in a glorious kind of entertainment,' says Cobain.
55 'That's not the future, that's happening *now*'.

Those who look on technology as an essential part of their lives but are getting bored with living
60 on a diet of computer games will jump at the chance to be part of this exciting new development.

If you are looking for the ultimate rock experience, contact
65 Future Sound of London via the Internet on FSOL<@fsol. demon. co.uk> today. Don't put it off till later!

8 You are a journalist. You have read about **FSOL** and you decide to do a feature on them. Read the article again and complete your notes.

Feature on phone gigs
1 – Arrange interview with group
Name –
Names of members –
Internet address –
2 – Talk to US gallery
Name –
City –
(Phone international directory
enquiries for number)
Background facts to remember
FSOL unique because
Music transmitted – how?
Audiences soon take part in real
concerts? No –

Vocabulary

9 Read the article again. Find words for the clues.

1 The place where the band actually play their music: their _ _ _ _ _ O
2 The name of the international computer network: _ N _ _ _ _ _ _
3 The pictures the audience watched at the concert in New York were lifelike or _ _ _ _ _ - _ _ _ _ _ _ _ _ _ _ L
4 Pictures created on a computer are called computer _ R _ _ _ _ _ _
5 In order to take part in concerts, fans will access information via computer _ _ _ K _ _ _ _ _ _ _ _

10 Make a list of seven phrasal verbs in the article.

Grammar

> ## Phrasal verbs 1
>
> ### 1 Phrasal verb + object – separable
>
> They **switched on** the computer workstation.
> They **switched** the computer workstation **on**.
> They **switched it on**.
>
> **But:**
>
> They ~~switched the computer workstation in the New York art gallery on.~~ ✗
> *Other separable verbs:* bring about, put off
>
> ### 2 Phrasal verb + object – inseparable
>
> Some people **look on** technology as an essential part of their lives.
> Some people **look on it** as an essential part of their lives.
> *Other inseparable verbs:* look for, look after, live on

Vision of Danger

🔊 EPISODE FOUR

1 **In Episode Three, what sort of feeling did Anya get in the park? What exactly did she and Stefan hear?**

2 **Read Episode Four and answer these questions.**

1 What did Stefan find out at the record shop?

2 Why do Anya and Stefan think they are hearing the song?

3 Who was Orpheus? Why was he special?

4 Why do Stefan and Anya think that Stone is in danger?

The next few days went quickly. Stefan and Anya met as often as they could. Anya shared her secret places in London with her new-
5 found friend and the days were long and warm. Their happiness was only occasionally spoiled by a sense of doom which neither of them could explain. They attributed it to the
10 thought of Stefan's return home at the end of the summer.

One morning, Stefan arrived at Anya's house somewhat agitated.

'You're late,' Anya said. 'Is
15 anything the matter?'

'I went to Tower Records on my way here. I wanted
20 to surprise you with that song we keep hearing all the time.' It was
25 true, every-where they went they heard the strange song
30 from the park. 'But you won't believe this,' Stefan continued. 'That record doesn't exist!'

'But we hear it everywhere!' Anya
35 exclaimed.

'Well, I asked for it in several shops and they looked at me as if I was mad. They said Stone had never recorded a song about Orpheus,'
40 Stefan explained.

'Well, we didn't imagine it!' Anya said. 'Or did we?'

'No, we didn't, but what if we are the only ones who can hear it?'
45 Stefan said.

'Yes, that's it! Maybe the words are trying to tell us something,' said Anya.

They went into her father's over-
50 stuffed library and looked through some books about mythology.

'Listen to this,' Anya said after a while. '"Orpheus. In mythology he was a wonderful musician. Even wild
55 animals and birds would stay to listen to him." Then it says how he lost his wife for ever in Hades, the land of the dead.'

'OK, but what does all that *mean?*'
60 said Stefan.

Suddenly, they both exclaimed: 'Stone! *He's* a wonderful musician. He must be in danger. We have to warn him!'

3 **What must Stefan and Anya do now? How will they find Stone? Do you think it will be easy? Why (not)?**

11 **Fill in the blanks with the correct form of the phrasal verbs in the article.**

1 I'm *looking for* my new Walkman. I don't know where I left it. Have you seen it?

2 Let's send this message by e-mail. Just let me ____ the computer.

3 I can't go out tonight. I have to ____ my little brother.

4 Computers have ____ a revolution in communications.

5 I love sweet food: I could ____ chocolate!

6 They had to ____ the game because of the rain.

7 I ____ schoolwork as something I have to do. It's not always fun!

Which sentences have a separable phrasal verb? Rewrite them using a pronoun instead of the object.

Listening

12 🔊 **Listen to two people talk about pop concerts. What four phrases do they use to talk about their preferences?**

Get talking

13 **Work in groups of 4–5. You have been offered half price tickets to either a traditional or a virtual reality concert, provided the whole group attends the same concert. Can you agree on which to go to or would you prefer to do your own thing and pay the full price?**

Revision

Reading

1 'Express' means something that is very fast. It is also a common name for newspapers. What do you think 'Children's Express' means? Think about the words and look at the photograph.
Scan the article to check your answer. (Don't worry about the blanks.)

Today's cub reporters, tomorrow's newshounds

Zumon Chowdhury, thirteen, talks with a confidence which would have been impossible
5 nine months ago. 'I interviewed the chief executive of _____ Football Association, Graham Kelly,' he says. Zumon and his fellow
10 reporters wanted to do _____ article on him. 'We did the research in a group and thought of the questions together. Then we wrote up
15 _____ article.' Before joining, Zumon had been getting average marks in English. 'My English in school has really improved and so has my
20 reading. Each time I do _____ interview I become more sure of myself.'

Zumon is one of the forty-five British children aged 8–18
25 who work for Children's Express, _____ only news agency run by children and designed to reflect their view of the society they live in.
30 Children's Express volunteers train as reporters and editors; they go out interviewing, hunting down stories and writing them up for
35 publication. Cathryn Atkinson, who is the London bureau director, briefs _____ children, edits their work and attempts to have it placed
40 in local and national newspapers. Children's Express, which was founded in the US in 1975, now has work published across the
45 country.

Fifteen-year-old Clency Lebrasse joined because one of his teachers suggested it. 'I spent a lot of time hanging out
50 before I joined,' he explains. These days he spends as much time as he can fit around homework at the bureau. 'I like doing sports stories most
55 – I feel passionately about how football corruption affects _____ kids and the problems they encounter when starting a football
60 career.'

Rachel Bulford, fourteen, joined Children's Express in order to get experience in journalism, the career she's
65 interested in. She had been looking for a way to get experience when a friend of hers told her about _____ Express. She applied
70 immediately. 'I've learnt a lot about how the press works, how to ask questions and to conduct myself,' she says. 'So far I've worked on _____ stor
75 exploring whether under-ag people can buy _____ lotter tickets.'

'Children's Express is doin something very importan
80 in giving children a chanc to give their perspectiv on _____ daily events to write on issues that th are concerned about,' sa
85 Cathryn Atkinson. '_____ agency is also helping t children to feel they have voice which deserves to heard.'

2 **Run your eyes over the text and find which paragraph (1–5) is about:**

1 what Children's Express is/does.
2 a girl who joined the agency with the purpose of learning about journalism.
3 why the agency is important.
4 a boy who has acquired a lot of self-confidence.
5 a boy whose habits have been changed by the agency.

EXAMPLE: 1 *paragraph 2*

3 **Read the article. Find the topic sentence of each paragraph.**

EXAMPLE: *paragraph 2: (Children's Express is the) only news agency run by children and designed to reflect their view of the society they live in.*

4 **Read the article again. Fill in the blanks with *the*, *a* or *an* where necessary.**

EXAMPLE: . . . of *the* Football Association.

5 **What do you call:**

1 corruption in football?
2 stories about sports?
3 a career in football?
4 an agency which deals with news?
5 schoolwork that you do at home (one word)?
6 the association of football clubs, players and others?

EXAMPLE: 1 *football corruption*

Check your answers by finding the words in the text.

6 **Rewrite these sentences using the phrases in brackets. The meaning must remain the same.**

1 Journalism is the career she's interested in. (in which)
2 One of his teachers suggested he join the agency. (teacher of)
3 The reporters can write on issues that they are concerned about. (about which)
4 Zumon Chowdhury has been working for the agency for nine months. He feels a lot better about his English. (who has)
5 Rachel Bulford joined the agency in order to get experience in journalism. (so that)

7 **You would like to be a foreign correspondent at Children's Express. Write a formal letter to the agency asking if it would be possible and what you would need to do next.**

Listening

8 🖥 **Listen to Amanda, a Children's Express reporter, doing interviews for an article for the local newspaper.**

a) What is the general topic?
b) Listen again. Tick (✔) the aspects of the topic the speakers mention.

- flower beds
- broken glass
- benches
- trees
- overgrown grass
- ice cream shop
- drinking fountains
- play equipment

c) Listen again. Which speaker (older man, teenage girl, little girl, little boy) thinks:
1 people like her have a greater need for a park?
2 children don't look after the park?
3 there needs to be more play equipment?
4 there should be a youth club in the park?
5 there should be an ice cream shop?

9 **Look at the picture of the park. What needs doing/needs to be done? What does the local council need to do?**

EXAMPLE: *The grass needs cutting.*

The wider world

10 In Britain, local councils provide communities with public amenities such as parks, sports centres and youth clubs. What about your country?

1 Who provides local amenities?
2 What amenities are there for the different age groups in your community?
3 Do you think there are enough amenities? What else would you like to see?

Project

11 In groups, devise a plan to renovate a local park or strip of land.

a) Identify a park or strip of land in your area which you feel is run-down or under-used.
b) Each of the members of the group briefly interviews five people to find out what they would like to see on the land if there was money available. Make sure you include different age groups (children, teenagers, adults).
c) Share the information with the rest of the group and consider the suggestions. Produce a report with recommendations that would make at least two of the age groups happy.

Grammar practice

1 Rewrite the sentences using a more informal register. (Unit 7)

EXAMPLE: 1 *Buffalo Bill was the cowboy Annie most liked working with.*
1 Buffalo Bill was the cowboy with whom Annie most liked working.
2 Arthur found the stone into which Merlin had stuck the magic sword.
3 The egg-shaped aircraft was the invention with which Monsieur Sauvant was most happy.
4 In the camps there are trained leaders to whom you can talk.
5 U2 are the group with whom I would most like to play in a virtual reality concert.
6 Basia is the Polish girl from whom the International Conservation Scouts got a letter.

2 Rewrite the pairs of sentences as one single sentence. (Unit 7)

EXAMPLE: 1 *Odysseus, who was a brave and skilful warrior, blinded the Cyclops to save his men.*

1 Odysseus blinded the Cyclops to save his men. Odysseus was a brave and skilful warrior.
2 His adventures are the central theme of the Odyssey. The Odyssey begins some years after the fall of Troy.
3 Orpheus went down to the Underworld and sang to Hades. Orpheus had the gift of music and song.
4 Thor was the greatest enemy of the giants. The giants were also hated and feared by humans.
5 Among Thor's chief enemies was the serpent Jörmungand. Jörmungand was the symbol of evil.

3 Put the verbs in brackets in the correct tense, Past Perfect Continuous or Past Simple. (Unit 8)

1 That evening, I _had been ringing_ (ring) him every ten minutes without success. I finally _decided_ (decide) to give up and go to bed.
2 Mira _____ (be) very tired when she arrived for dinner because she _____ (play) tennis all day.
3 Poor David! He _____ (study) History for five hours when he _____ (realise) that next day's exam was Science.
4 Annie Oakley _____ (work) in Wild West shows for some time when Buffalo Bill _____ (ask) her to join his show.
5 Jason _____ (buy) video games for a long time before he _____ (get) fed up with computers.

4 Police officer Notu Bright has been given a robber's exact description by the many witnesses. He has several suspects. Help him identify the robber. (Unit 10)

Witnesses' details: Male, aged about 35, approximately 1.80 metres tall, very thin, can't weigh more than 70 kg
EXAMPLE: *It can't be suspect 1. He's not tall enough.*
Suspect 1: Male, aged 35, 1.61 metres tall, 70 kg
Suspect 2: Male, 55 years old, 1.88 metres tall, 75 kg
Suspect 3: Male, 27, 1.85 metres tall, 90 kg
Suspect 4: Male, 35 years of age, 1.82 metres tall, 69.5 kg

5 Someone has just left a large amount of money to your school. The money will be used to improve the building and amenities and the school authorities have asked for your suggestions on things which need to be done.

a) Make notes about the modifications and the purpose of each.
EXAMPLE:

Modification	Purpose
– build commonroom	– students can chat to friends after class
– paint classrooms	– provide more pleasant learning atmosphere

b) Write four sentences explaining who needs to make the modifications and four where the agent is not important. Explain the purpose of the improvement. (Units 10 and 11)
EXAMPLE: *The school authorities need to build a commonroom so that students can go and chat to their friends after class. The classrooms need painting in order to provide a more pleasant learning atmosphere.*

6 Fill in the spaces with the correct form of the phrasal verbs in the box. (Unit 11)

> look on   put off   bring about   switch on
> look for

1 Rachel Bulford _____ Children's Express as a valuable way of building towards a career in journalism.
2 Working for Children's Express has _____ many changes for the young reporters.
3 The young reporter _____ the computer as soon as she arrived at the Children's Express office.
4 Hugh _____ doing his homework, but he's always ready to write articles.
5 Before he joined Children's Express, Clency Lebrasse had been _____ something to do after school.

Change the word order of the sentences which contain a separable transitive verb.

Grammar

1 use defining relative clauses with prepositions to give important information. (Unit 7)
2 use non-defining relative clauses to add extra information. (Unit 7)
3 talk about actions which lasted or were repeated before a point in the past by using the Past Perfect Continuous. (Unit 8)
4 talk about things that belong to people, animals or other things by using a possessive form. (Unit 8)
5 use or omit the articles *the* and *a/an*. (Unit 9)
6 express purpose using *(in order) to*, *in order not to*, *so as not to* and *so (that)*. (Unit 10)
7 use *too* and *enough* to talk about whether a quality is sufficient or not. (Unit 10)
8 talk about things which it is necessary to do using *need . . .* (Unit 11)
9 use separable and inseparable phrasal verbs. (Unit 11)

Skills

READING

● concentrate on important information first. (Unit 7)
● identify topic sentences. (Unit 8)
● find specific information quickly. (Unit 10)

WRITING

● write a formal letter. (Unit 9)
● write biographies. (Unit 10)

LISTENING

● concentrate on key words first. (Unit 7)
● listen to conversations in an intelligent way. (Unit 9)

SPEAKING

● narrate myths and legends. (Unit 10)
● express your preferences. (Unit 11)

What's on the box?

1 **Could you manage without television? Why (not)? Which television programme would you miss the most? Which programme would you not miss at all? Tell your partner. Are your opinions similar?**

Reading

2 **Read the text opposite to find this information:**

1 Keanu Reeves's former occupation in the film *Speed*.
2 the date when Mickey Mouse was 'born'.
3 what *The Private Life of Plants* is about this week.
4 where the new teacher works in *Hearts and Minds*.
5 what time *Neighbours* is on.
6 why *Gladiators* is special this week.

> ⭐ *A review tells you what a critic thinks about a play, a film, a book or a television programme. When you read a review look for words and phrases that tell you the author's attitude.*

3 **Answer the questions about the television guide.**

1 What is the film *Speed* like? How do we know?
2 Is *Neighbours* worth watching? How do we know?
3 Does the critic like *Homage to Mickey*? How do we know?
4 What does the reviewer think *Hearts and Minds* is going to be like? How do we know?
5 Are the groups and singers in *Top of the Pops* important? How do we know?
6 Does the critic think *Gladiators* is going to be good? How do we know?

Staying in: Pick of the day

CHANNEL 1

5 **Top of the Pops**
Seventies special: Abba, Queen, The Doors, Jimmy Hendrix and many other rock classics.
7.00–7.45

10 **The Private Life of Plants**
Last in this excellent series. How do plants survive? Tonight, we travel the world to find out. Great photography. **9.00–10.00**

15 **CHANNEL 2**

Neighbours Omnibus
For those who have missed life with the Neighbours this week, a chance to watch all five episodes.
20 Annalise reveals some dark secrets and we finally discover what's bothering her. All in all an eventful week for the residents of Ramsey Street. **6.00–7.15**

25 **Hearts and Minds**
1/4. Promising start to this schoolroom saga. An idealistic new teacher arrives at an inner city school and tries to make poetry
30 interesting for his unruly students.
9.30–10.30

CHANNEL 3

Homage to Mickey
A rare opportunity to see the best
35 of Mickey Mouse animation from his creation in 1928 to the present day. Good old-fashioned fun.
5.00–6.00

Gladiators
40 The Gladiators give members of the public a good run for their money in more exciting competitions of strength and speed. Don't miss the final of this year's series of the
45 ever popular show. **7.15–8.00**

CHANNEL 4

Panorama
Are girls better language learners than boys? Do girls get better
50 results in all-girls schools? Join the team of investigative reporters and find out. Interesting – and surprising – findings. **7.00–7.50**

Moviedrome: Speed
55 Keanu Reeves stars as an ex-cop trying to stop a bomb from going off on a bus. Nail-biting action guaranteed to keep you on the edge of your seat. **8.00–10.00**

Grammar

> ## Present Simple as future
>
> **Definite future plans and arrangements**
>
> Anna **leaves** for Paris tonight at 8.00.
> *She doesn't do this every night. She is definitely going to do it tonight.*
>
> **Look!**
> **I'm staying up** late **tonight** to watch a film on television.
> *I have decided to do it: it's a definite **personal** future plan.*
>
> A new drama **starts tonight.** It sounds promising.
> *It's not the reviewer's plan. It has been programmed and the reviewer is talking about the **timetable** of programmes.*

4 Read the sentences. Do they refer to general time or to the future? Mark the sentences **G** (general time) or **F** (future).

1 What time does your train leave this afternoon? *F*
2 What time do you usually leave for school?
3 The news usually starts at 9.00 but tonight it starts at 9.15 because there is a special programme on before.
4 Tonight flight 302 from Athens arrives at 6.05. We'd better hurry: it's already 5.55!
5 What time does the film end this evening? My Dad wants to pick us up afterwards.
6 Banks open at 9.00 and close at 3.30.

5 Complete the sentences with the correct form, Present Simple or Present Continuous, of the verbs in brackets.

1 What ____ (happen) in next week's *Hearts and Minds*? The teacher ____ (leave) the school but the students learn to like poetry!
2 What time ____ the match ____ (start) tonight? I ____ (watch) it with John. Do you want to watch it with us?
3 The new video shop ____ (open) today. I ____ (meet) my friend there this afternoon.
4 What time ____ this plane ____ (land)? I can hardly wait to get off.

Listening

6 🖃 Listen to the conversation. Answer the questions.

1 Which programmes in the television guide are mentioned in the conversation?
2 What do the speakers each want to watch?

7 🖃 Listen to the conversation again. Complete the sentences.

1 Nicola wants to watch *Top of the Pops* because . . . . . .
2 Claire doesn't want to watch *Gladiators:* she . . . . . .
3 Eddy then agrees with . . . . . .
4 Eddy thinks *Gladiators* is going to be exciting because . . . . . .
5 Nicola is not happy. She thinks they . . . . . .
6 Their mother doesn't want them to . . . . . .

How do they solve their disagreement?

Get talking

8 Get ready to solve a problem.

a) 🖃 Listen to the conversation in Exercise 6 again. Write down
   1 one way of asking for a suggestion.
   2 three ways of making suggestions.
   3 three ways of rejecting suggestions.
   4 one way of compromising.
   EXAMPLE: 1 *What shall we watch?*

b) Read the television guide again. Circle the programmes you would like to watch.

c) Make groups of four. Together, decide what programmes you are going to watch. You only have one television!
   Use the expressions in a) to find the best solution for everyone.

9 Read the titles of these reviews of *Gladiators*. Which reviewer do you think likes the programme? Which doesn't?

Read the reviews to check your answers.

10 Answer these questions about the reviews.

1 What do you have to do to win these games: Pursuit, Hit and Run and Pole-Axe?

2 What skills do you (think you) need to have to play the games in question 1?

3 What do these expressions mean? Are they favourable or unfavourable?
  'You've seen it all before.'
  'The programme has been getting bigger and better.'
  'Watch *Gladiators*, if you must . . .'
  'The *Gladiators* are back for more of the same.'

Contenders, ready? Gladiators, ready? Viewers, ready for more of the same?

The *Gladiators* are back for more of the same: grown-ups in silly super-hero style costumes running, climbing,
5 jumping and punching each other like over-excited children in a high tech playground.

To be fair, there are a few additions to the show.
10 'Pursuit' is a new obstacle course. Contestants are given a head start on the Gladiators: they leap over obstacles, vault over high bars and generally
15 run around with two Gladiators close behind them. The first contestant to sprint to the finishing line without being caught wins the event
20 and gets ten points. In 'Hit and Run', the contestants try to cross a suspension bridge without being knocked off by a big, heavy ball which the
25 Gladiators control. If all this sounds familiar it's because you've seen it all before, under a different name.

I, personally, don't
30 understand the popularity of the programme but 15 million fans up and down the country love it. If you happen to be one of them, the return of the
35 series will have you somersaulting with joy.

Watch *Gladiators*, if you must, on Saturdays at 7.15 on Channel 3.

The Gladiators are back!

Ever since the first series of *Gladiators* burst onto our screens three years ago, the programme has been getting
5 bigger and better with more Gladiators and even more sensational events to test the strengths and skills of contenders and Gladiators
10 alike.

Last year's series was a great success but the makers of the programme were determined not to rest on
15 their laurels, so they set out to add new, exciting games.

The new events are hair-raising and will have you cheering in your sitting room.
20 In 'Pole-Axe', for example, Gladiator and contender race up individual 10 metre poles which have pegs sticking out of them. The first to climb to
25 the top slams their hand down on a button which pulls in the pegs of the opponent's pole. Speed,
30 balance and a good head for heights are essential for this event.
35 *Gladiators* provides good, wholesome entertainment
40 for all the family. It is ingenious, exciting and always fun. It belongs in a category of its own.

You can watch *Gladiators*
45 every Saturday at 7.15 on Channel 3.

Grammar

Verbs which cannot usually be used in the continuous form

1 Feelings
15 million fans up and down the country **love** it.
(*Also*: appreciate, hate, like, mind, want, wish)

2 Perception
All this **sounds** familiar.
(*Also*: feel, hear, notice, observe, see, smell)

3 Mental activity
I **think** *Gladiators* is a really good programme.
(*It is my opinion.*)
(*Also*: agree, believe, know, mean, realise, remember, think (=believe), understand.)

4 Possession
Gladiators **belongs** in a category of its own.
(*Also*: belong to, have (got), owe, own, possess)

Look!
I'm **thinking of** going to watch the *Gladiators* live. (*I'm planning.*)
What **are** you **thinking about**? (*No opinion is asked for.*)
I'm **having** a good time. (*I'm enjoying myself.*)

---

11 Complete these sentences with the Present Continuous or the Present Simple of the verbs in brackets.

1 This film is very confusing. _____ you _____ (understand) what's going on?
2 What do you think of the party? _____ you _____ (have) a good time?
3 It _____ (feel) very strange to be at school on a Sunday.
4 I _____ (think) they _____ (have) lunch. It _____ (smell) very good!
5 Sarah's telling everyone she's going to be on TV. _____ you _____ (believe) her?
6 Let's change channels. I _____ (think) this programme is really boring.

12 Prepare to enter a 'Pick of the day' competition.

a) In pairs, make up an evening of television programmes that you would really like to watch. Write a 'Pick of the day' like that on page 54.
b) Pair A: Turn to page 103.
  Pair B: Turn to page 105.

---

1 **What do Anya and Stefan think the song about Orpheus means?**

2 **Read Episode Five and answer these questions.**
1 How do Stefan and Anya manage to find Stone's address?
2 Why couldn't they speak to him?
3 Why did Anya fall out of the tree?

Vision of Danger

EPISODE FIVE

It was proving impossible to get Stone's address. Then Stefan had a brilliant idea: posing as a reporter for a teenage magazine, he managed to
5 set up an appointment with Stone's agent. Once Stefan was at her office, Anya phoned and got the agent to leave the room for a few minutes. That gave Stefan enough time to find
10 Stone's address from his agent's files.
  Stone's place was in the middle of the country and it was almost invisible from the road. It was surrounded by thick, high walls. The
15 gate was guarded by two security men with large, fierce dogs and small cameras were filming everything.
  'We've come to see Stone,' Stefan
20 said to one of the men.
  'You and everybody else! Just go to his concert,' the man said unpleasantly.
  'You don't understand,' said Anya.
25 'We *have* to talk to him. This is really important.'
  'Yes, yes. That's what they all say. Now be a good girl and go away,' the second man said.
30 Anya's face flushed with anger. She and Stefan were now even more determined to see the star.
  They walked round the walls surrounding Stone's house and found
35 a tall oak tree. If they could just climb up the tree without being detected by the security system . . ..
  As they started to climb, a firm hand gripped Stefan's ankle. It was one of
40 the security guards. Stefan came down with a crash. He could see the dogs' sharp white teeth as they barked and growled at him. Anya was startled and lost her footing,
45 following Stefan down.
  'I've just about had enough of you two. Now clear off or I'll set the dogs on you!' shouted the security guard.
  Terrified, Anya and Stefan leapt up
50 and started to run. They didn't stop until the sound of the fierce, angry dogs had died away. But the words of the song were still ringing loudly and insistently in their ears.

3 **Why do you think the words of the song rang loudly and insistently in Anya and Stefan's ears? What do you think they will do next? What would you do?**

Just the job

1 **Which of these jobs would you like to do the most? Number them in order of preference.**

- dentist
- teacher
- newsreader
- photographer
- archeologist
- artist

Compare your answers with your partner. Explain your choices.

Listening

⭐ *When you have missed the beginning of a conversation, you can still guess what the speakers are talking about. To do this:*
1. *Try to pick out key words in order to guess the topic of conversation.*
2. *Try to make deductions about what was said before.*

2 📼 **Listen. Match the conversations with the jobs in Exercise 1.**

EXAMPLE: 1 – *newsreader*

3 📼 **Listen again. How do you think the conversations started? For each one, write one or two questions that the people were probably asked first.**

A short while ago, Nick Moss was an ordinary schoolboy. Now he's a well-paid model who gets 35 constant offers of work.

5 His is the kind of success story which fuels the imagination of thousands of young people round the world. Nick hadn't really considered becoming a 10 model. It all started quite by chance when he was spotted by his sister Kate's modelling agency. Kate Moss is one of the best-paid models in the world. The agency 15 took some photographs of Nick and 'things just took off straight away,' he says, still sounding surprised.

But success stories like Nick's are 20 rare. If you think a modelling career depends on looks alone, you're in for a disappointment.

'I wasn't a handsome kid and I don't think I've got much better 25 with age,' says Nick modestly. 'I've just got the 'in' look.' However, it's not just looks. But providing you have personality as well, things could turn out the 30 same way for you.

Looks and personality: is that the full story, then? Meet Tracy. She's a charismatic fifteen-year-old with looks to die for. But her perfect face has never adorned the pages of fashion magazines. 'You have to have a good photo portfolio and also belong to a really good, professional agency,' 40 she says. You also have to be resilient: Tracy has applied for over a dozen jobs and has been rejected as many times. But she hasn't let this get her down too 45 much: 'I'm giving myself another year,' says Tracy. 'Unless I get something soon, I'll give up on the idea of modelling.'

So would things have been as 50 easy for Nick if his sister hadn't been a famous model herself? Who knows? If she hadn't been a famous model, perhaps he wouldn't have been spotted.

55 Nick Moss hasn't let sudden fame go to his head and is realistic about the limitations of a modelling career. 'Modelling's fun but it doesn't last forever,' 60 says Nick. So you won't be disappointed as long as you realise it could all end as suddenly as it started.

Reading

4 **What is it like to be a model, do you think? Write notes in the chart.**

Modelling	
physical requirements:	
other requirements:	
negative aspects of the job:	

Read the article on the opposite page. Check and add to your answers.

5 **Read this summary of the text. There are six pieces of information which are wrong. Underline the mistakes and rewrite the summary using the correct information.**

This text is about modelling. Several young models talk about their modelling careers. The single most important thing in modelling is to have good looks. It is also important to have a good agent, a good portfolio and to have a model in the family. Nick Moss explains that his sister became a famous model when his agency spotted her. Not all models are as lucky as Nick and some have to wait for a long time to get a job: Tracy was once on the cover of a fashion magazine but she hasn't worked since. Modelling is a disappointing occupation.

6 **In pairs, think of a title for the article.**

Grammar

Conditional sentences without *if*.

Unless I get something soon, I'll give up on the idea of modelling.
*If I **don't** get something soon, I'll give up on the idea of modelling. That's definite.*

Provided/providing (that) you have personality as well, things could turn out the same way for you.
*Things might turn out the same way for you if, **but only if**, you have personality as well.*

My parents would let me become a model **as long as** I continued my studies too.
*My parents would let me become a model if, **but only if**, I continued my studies too.*

---

7 **Rewrite these sentences using *provided/providing (that), unless* or *as long as*.**

1 I'll help you with your maths only if you help me with my English.
2 If you don't have a good portfolio you won't get a modelling job.
3 You can still apply for the job but only if you send your application form in today.
4 If you don't like working with children, don't become a teacher.
5 This camera's very simple. Your photos will be pretty good – but only if you don't point the camera at the sun.
6 I would only agree to share a room with my sister if she promised not to take my things.

8 **Read the questions. They are all about things which would not be a good idea in normal circumstances.**

a) Answer the questions using conditional sentences.
EXAMPLE: *I would jump out of a window if the room was on fire and provided that the window was on the ground floor!*

In what circumstances would you . . .
1 . . . jump out of a window?
2 . . . pretend to be someone else?
3 . . . lie to your best friend?
4 . . . kill an animal?
5 . . . disobey your parents?
6 . . . go out with the boy/girl your friend likes?

b) Make groups of four. Read out your answers from a). For each question, decide whose answer is the most logical or sensible.

9 You are a detective. Look at the picture of the tomb carefully. What can you guess about the person's life?

Reading

10 Read the text and check your guesses in Exercise 9.

> ✴ Words like **this, it** or **he** connect different parts of a text. They may refer to a word, a phrase, a sentence, or several sentences in another part of the text. Understanding what these words refer to will help you understand the text better.

11 Find out what these words refer to.

1 it   (l.2) *the picture*
2 he   (l.16)
3 he   (l.18)
4 that (l.23)
5 their (l.33)
6 that (l.52)
7 this (l.70)
8 it   (l.87)

Vocabulary

12 Look at the picture in the text. Label the numbered parts with words from the text. Why are these things important for the archeologist?

EXAMPLE: 1 – *skeleton; the position may tell us something about the culture's beliefs*

13 Read the text again. In your own words, write a short paragraph about the person in the tomb.

Digging up the past

Look at this picture. To you and me, it is just a rather scary scene which doesn't tell us much about the person
5 buried here. But the expert eye of an archeologist can find enough clues to tell us a lot about this person.

Matthew is an expert on
10 Amerindian cultures. He looks at the tomb carefully for a couple of minutes and then says: 'This is the tomb of a man, probably a rich,
15 important warrior. And I'm almost sure that he didn't die of natural causes.'

How can he tell? 'Easy,' Matthew explains. 'Do you
20 see that line on the side of the skull? That's where the skull was broken by something very heavy. That's probably what killed him. If
25 this man had died of natural causes, the skull wouldn't have that fracture.'

The contents of the tomb help Matthew determine the
30 occupation and even the rank of the person. In some cultures, people used to bury

the dead with some of their belongings and sometimes
35 even with dishes of their favourite foods. 'If the man hadn't been rich and important, he wouldn't have owned those fantastic
40 jewels,' says Matthew. 'The large piece of gold jewellery is in fact something warriors wore over their chests for protection in battle.'
45 Like a detective, Matthew analyses the remains and finally comes up with a complete picture of the culture to which the man
50 belonged.

'The position of the skeleton is like that of a baby in his mother,' Matthew points out. 'From this we can
55 deduce that in this man's culture death was seen as a new birth, the beginning of a new life.' From looking at the pelvis, he knows it's a man: if
60 it had been a woman, the cavity would be larger. And from the wear on his teeth Matthew can guess that he was around thirty when he

4

died and that his diet probably consisted of meat and hard vegetables: if he had eaten just vegetables his teeth wouldn't be so worn.

All this is amazing but it is only the beginning. Once the archeologists have all the information they can get, they pass it on to computer engineers. Using software originally designed for nuclear power stations, the engineers feed the information into a computer, like pieces of a gigantic puzzle.

Then if you press the correct keys on the keyboard, the screen lights up and the old pyramids, the people and their towns and villages appear before your eyes. 'It's certainly a very exciting new development,' says Matthew. 'It's the final step towards really bringing the past back to life!'

Grammar

Talking about conditions in the past

1 The man was rich and important. ⟶ He owned fantastic jewels.

   Imagined past condition   *Imagined past consequence*

   If + *Past Perfect* + would(n't) have + *Past Participle*

If the man **hadn't been** rich and important, he **wouldn't have owned** those fantastic jewels.

But he was rich and important so he did own fantastic jewels.

2 He didn't eat just vegetables ⟶ His teeth are worn now.

   Imagined past condition   *Imagined present consequence*

   If + *Past Perfect* + would(n't) + *infinitive*

If he **had eaten** just vegetables, his teeth **wouldn't be** so worn now.

But he didn't eat just vegetables, so now his teeth are worn.

---

14 **Write conditional sentences with the pairs of sentences.**

EXAMPLE: 1 *If he hadn't dug up his garden, he wouldn't have found treasure.*

1 He dug up his garden. He found treasure buried there.
2 He reported his discovery to the police. He didn't get to keep the treasure.
3 Mark did badly at school. Now he has to have private lessons.
4 Chris didn't go to the museum with his school because he was ill. Now he doesn't have the information he needs for his project.
5 Lucia went to Egypt. She had a chance to see the Pyramids.
6 Cousteau invented a small submersible. Now it is possible for archeologists to look for sites at the bottom of the sea.
7 Carla's father was very keen on history. He often told her stories about ancient civilisations. Now Carla is a historian.

15 **Think of past events in your life which you remember well. What consequences did they have? Write notes under the headings.**

Memorable events in my life		Their consequences
7 years old: pulled dog's tail	⟶	*dog bit me. Had to have stitches*
had argument with friend	⟶	*now not friends any more*

Use your notes to write conditional sentences.

EXAMPLE: *If I hadn't pulled the dog's tail, it wouldn't have bitten me and I wouldn't have had to have stitches.*

Get talking

16 **Have you found a wonderful piece of treasure?**

Student A: Turn to page 103.
Student B: Turn to page 105.

A slice of life

1 Think of people you met in your childhood whom you remember well, for example a kind friend, a horrible neighbour or a funny relative. Why do you remember them so well? Tell your partner.

Word watch

✦ *Some words which we use for descriptions have similar meanings so they are sometimes confused.*

2 Write these words under the correct heading.

> thin (person) fat slim (person) skinny wide plump overweight high tall big little small large low short narrow heavy

weight   height   width   overall size
skinny

3 Use some of the words in Exercise 2 to complete these sentences. Look the words up in your dictionary if you are not sure.

1 A: I'd like to lose some weight.
   B: Why? You're not _____ (a).
   A: Don't be so polite. The word is fat.
   B: I think you're _____ (b), – you haven't got a weight problem at *all*. You don't want to be _____ (c) like those models in magazines, do you? They're so thin they look ill.
   A: They do not! They're just lovely and _____ (d).

2 A: How _____ (a) are you?
   B: Why?
   A: Can you get my cat down from the top of the kitchen cupboard?
   B: Well, how _____ (b) is the cupboard?
   A: About 3 metres.
   B: Then I'm too _____ (c) to reach it. And I don't like standing on ladders.
   A: Silly cat! Why couldn't it have gone on the bookshelf? At least that's _____ (d) and I can reach it easily.

Reading

4 Look at the picture carefully.

a) In three minutes, write as many words as you can to describe as many of the people as you can. Compare your words with your partner. Who wrote the most words? Who described the most people?

b) Read the text on page 63. Which of the people in the picture are described? Did you use similar words to describe them?

5 Read the text again. Mark each sentence True or False.

1 The children in the story were scared of Nieves because he was a very odd stranger.
2 The madman, the ballet teacher and the twins scared them too.
3 Nieves chased the author one evening.
4 The author's parents were amongst the first to trust Nieves.
5 The author's neighbour didn't trust Nieves.
6 She was right not to trust him.
7 In the end Nieves became like everybody else.

He walked heavily down the road in the quiet of the early afternoon. In the blazing sun he roamed the narrow twisting streets of the town. He was laughing and holding a conversation with an invisible person.

5 'Here he comes! Here he comes!' we children whispered so we wouldn't wake the adults from their afternoon nap. Through half open shutters we watched him go by, shuddering with excitement and fear.

10 The object of our curiosity was Nieves, a mysterious plump middle-aged man. His skin was rough and tanned and his eyes were like pieces of coal in pools of snow. When he spoke, his white teeth gleamed through fleshy red lips.

15 As in most places, there was in our town a collection of funny characters: the cheerful chubby madman who was nearly bald and drove an imaginary car down the street; the eccentric old ballet teacher who danced in her garden in long bright flowing

20 dresses; and the strange twins, pale and skinny, in their white dresses. They stood stiffly on their verandah and watched us other kids play through their sad dark eyes.

But Nieves was different: he was new to our town.

25 None of us knew where he had come from or where exactly he lived now. And he was clearly mad!

'He must be from another planet,' my cousin suggested breathlessly.

'Don't be silly! There are no people on other
30 planets. I think his boat was shipwrecked and he managed to swim to the beach. All his family died and he's gone mad from the pain.'

One evening, as I walked home from running an errand, I heard heavy steps behind me. Gathering all
35 my courage, I looked round to see Nieves a short distance away, smiling his big white smile. I ran home as fast as I could, occasionally turning to see if he was still there. He followed me all the way home but I managed to get in just before he was able to reach
40 me. I slammed the door in his face and wailed as I pointed to the door. Alarmed, my mother opened the door.

'This is Mr Luna,' she said. 'He's going to work with your father at the boatyard. Please excuse my
45 daughter's behaviour,' she added turning to him. 'She has a vivid imagination.'

Nieves Luna soon became part of the family. At first, people criticised my parents for taking him into our home. 'The man is obviously a lunatic,' said the nosy
50 woman next door. 'It'll come to no good. I wouldn't let my children spend so much time with a mad stranger.' But Nieves was a kind friendly man who was very fond of children. He never lost the habit of talking to imaginary listeners but in time he was
55 accepted by the people in our town.

6 Answer these questions about the text.

1 Why do you think the twins watched the other children play 'through their sad dark eyes'?

2 Why was the author upset the evening she saw Nieves walking behind her?

3 How do you think the author's mother felt when she realised why her child was upset?

4 How do you think Nieves eventually became accepted in the town?

Grammar

Descriptions: sequence of adjectives

1	2	3	4	5
quality/opinion	size	age	shape	colour

6	7	8
-ed and -ing adjectives	origin	material NOUN

He roamed the **narrow twisting** streets of the town. *(4 + 6)*
She danced in the garden in **long bright flowing** dresses. *(2 + 5 + 6)*

This is only a guide. The order may vary according to the specific adjectives used and the speaker's intention.

7 Read the sentences and the adjectives. What type of information do the adjectives give?

1 When I was a child I used to play with a <u>boy</u>. (small *(size)*, Argentinian *(origin)*)

2 She's a beautiful <u>girl</u>. She could be a model. (tall, dark-haired)

3 There used to be a <u>tree</u> in our garden. (huge, wonderful, green)

4 We lived in a <u>house</u>. (stone, old, lovely)

5 My grandmother was a <u>lady</u>. (funny, Scottish)

6 She had a kind <u>face</u>. (round)

7 We were all excited when my father bought a <u>car</u>. (red, beautiful, American)

8 Rewrite the sentences using the adjectives with the nouns <u>underlined</u>. Be careful! Some of the sentences already have an adjective.

EXAMPLE: *When I was a child I used to play with a small Argentinian boy.*

Writing

⭐ *When you write a description of someone, write about the person's general appearance, give some details of physical characteristics which you think are important, and include some information about the person's character.*

9 **Read the excerpt from the story on page 63. Answer these questions.**

1 How many sentences does the author use to describe Nieves?
2 In what order does she write about:
  – Nieves's character?
  – his general appearance?
  – details of some of his physical characteristics?

> The object of our curiosity was Nieves, a mysterious plump middle-aged man. His skin was rough and tanned and his eyes were like pieces of coal in pools of snow. When he spoke, his white teeth gleamed through fleshy red lips . . . He was a kind friendly man who was very fond of children.

10 **Choose one of the people you told your partner about in Exercise 1.**

a) Write notes under the headings.

general appearance	physical details	character
tall	*curly hair*	*funny*

b) Tick (✓) the adjectives which are most important, in your opinion. Use these in c).
c) Write a description of your person following the order of the description of Nieves.
  EXAMPLE: *The person I remember most from my childhood is my grandmother. She was . . .*

Vocabulary

11 **Match the pictures with the words in the box.**

| mites   convict   garlic   freezer |

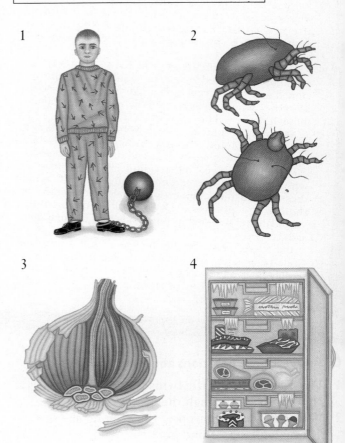

1
2
3
4

Reading

12 **Read the texts opposite. Match these titles with the texts.**

* Polar bear
* Prize jigsaw
* Baldman of Doncatraz
* Keep away, Lassie!

13 **Read the texts again. Answer these questions.**

1 How do you think the dustmen feel about keeping the money?
2 Do you think children will enjoy going to bed with their teddies if they follow the advice of the researchers? Why (not)?
3 Why is it a good idea for some dogs to eat mints?
4 Why is the story about the prisoner absurd?

It's a funny old world!

1 . . . . .
Two dustmen who found £3,500 thrown away as rubbish have been told that they can keep it. All they have to do now is to work out how to put the notes back together again: they are in 8,000 pieces and have to be reassembled.

2 . . . . . .
Mites live in the fur of teddy bears. Asthmatic children who breathe them in often get asthma attacks. But they don't have to give up their teddy bears any more. Researchers at Southampton University are advising them to put their teddies in the freezer before taking them to bed. The mites are killed by the cold.

15 **3** . . . . . .
Good news for dog owners: you don't have to keep your beloved pet away from you because of its bad breath. A company has just put canine mints on the market. The manufacturers expect sales of the sweets
20 to take off quickly because they discovered that many dogs have an ailment which makes their breath smell of garlic.

4 . . . . . .
A prisoner in Doncaster jail who was unhappy about
25 his prison haircut was given £100 compensation. He complained that they had taken off too much hair and that his new haircut made him look like a convict.

Grammar

> **Phrasal Verbs (2): verbs used with and without an object**
>
> **take off**
> Manufacturers expect sales of the sweets to **take off** quickly.
> (= to rise – no object after the phrasal verb)
> The prisoner complained that they had
> **taken off** too much hair. *or*
> **taken** too much hair **off.**
> (= to remove – object: too much hair)
> *Other examples:*
> **make up**
> 1 *to become friends again after a quarrel e.g.* We **made up** with a kiss.
> 2 *to invent a story/piece of information e.g.* I **made up** a story. *or* I **made** a story **up.**
> **give up**
> 1 *to stop trying to do something e.g.* I tried to understand the computer game but I **gave up** after a while.
> 2 *to stop having or doing something e.g.* I **gave up** chocolate. *or* I **gave** chocolate **up.**
> *For more examples look at page 109.*

14 **Complete the sentences with phrasal verbs from the text.**

1 Look at you! You're all muddy and wet. ____ ·your shoes before you come in.
2 Just as the plane was about to ____ I realised I had lost my bag.
3 – I can't _____ the solution to this problem.
– Don't _____. You can do it if you try harder.
4 If you really want to lose weight, you'll have to ____ sugary foods.
5 Wear a mask when you paint that wall. It's dangerous to ____ the fumes.

15 **Find people in your class who have done these activities. Ask them to tell you more about them (when and why, for example).**

1 made up an excuse for not doing their homework.
2 given up something they really like.
3 worked out in order to develop muscles.
4 worked out the solution to a difficult problem without any help.
5 had a quarrel with a friend and have never made up since.

Dreams and worries

1 Which of these are you most worried about? Number them from 1 (most worried about) to 10 (least worried about).

- your appearance
- school
- the environment
- your relationship with your family (parents, brothers and sisters)

- money
- boy/girl friendships
- your future
- your safety when you go out
- unemployment
- world poverty

Carry out a class survey to find out what worries people in your class the most. Use the above items.

2 Read the diary entries. Match the entries with the pictures.

Ariadne Matthews

1

26 March
Dear diary,
    We went to see the film George Harrison (my favourite Beatle!) made to raise funds
5 for the people in Bangladesh who are starving. The music was great but the pictures of all those skinny kids really breaks your heart. I wish we could do more to help them. The world can really be a
10 rotten place sometimes. I wish everybody had food to eat and money to spend. I wish there weren't any wars – ever!
    And I wish my parents would let me go to the concert in the park. All my friends
15 are going and besides, it's for a good cause. But mum and dad think it's dangerous. They worry too much! Trying to talk to your parents can be really frustrating sometimes!
20   And while I'm at it, I also wish my brother wouldn't take my things without asking! I can't find my Simon and Garfunkel tape. I'm sure he's pinched it again. Honestly, I've told him not to take my
25 things but he couldn't care less. Rat!

2

13 May
Mum and dad are really worried. They think we can't tell but the atmosphere is so tense you could cut it with a knife.
5 Apparently, dad's company are laying lots of people off because there isn't enough work. Could dad be made redundant too? If he loses his job, we can say goodbye to holidays and
10 birthday treats. I wish I knew what was going on.
    Got my project on the environment back and the teacher really liked it. I wish I could say the same about my
15 friends. They think I'm exaggerating and it makes me so mad. I wish they realised how bad the situation is: we went to the seaside for the bank holiday weekend and there was all this filthy
20 rubbish on the beach. All they worry about is boys. Though I admit they're a bit of a problem too: E. hasn't called!
    A.

5 **What do Aurora and Ariadne mean by the following expressions?**
1 . . . you could cut the atmosphere with a knife.
2 . . . while I'm at it . . .
3 . . . he couldn't care less.
4 I'm sure he's pinched it again.
5 . . . we can say goodbye to holidays . . .

Grammar

> **1 Complaining about or regretting present situations:** *wish (that)* **+ past tense**
> *There are wars in several parts of the world. You really dislike this but you can't do much to change the situation.*
> I **wish/If only** there **weren't** any wars.
>
> I **wish/If only** I **could do** more to help.
> *But I can't.*
>
> **2 Complaining about what other people do:** *wish (that)* **+** *would* **+ infinitive**
> *Aurora's brother is always taking her things. She wants him to stop doing it and she hopes he will.*
> She **wishes** her brother **wouldn't take** her things.

Aurora Davies

3 **Which of the things in Exercise 1 are Aurora and Ariadne worried about?**

4 **Make true sentences about Ariadne and Aurora. Use words from each column and complete the sentences with information from the text. Who can write the most sentences?**

Ariadne Aurora	angry frustrated impatient worried depressed	and because so but

EXAMPLE: *Ariadne is worried because her dad may lose his job.*

6 **Write sentences complaining about or regretting the things in Exercise 1.**

EXAMPLE: *I wish I was taller.*
I wish people wouldn't pollute the environment.

7 **Write wishes using** *wish* **+ past tense or** *wish* **+** *would.*
1 You're in an exam. You don't know any of the answers.
2 Your teacher always asks you questions in class. You'd like her to ask someone else for a change.
3 Your mum's always telling you off for watching television. You'd like her to stop.
4 You have to get up very early every day. You want to sleep late but you can't.
5 You see some clothes you really like but you can't afford them.
6 There's a film you want to see but you're not old enough.

8 **Look at your class survey in Exercise 1. How many people were worried about their relationship with their family? What kind of problems do they have? What was the most common problem?**

Reading

9 **Look at the photograph of a scene from the play, *A Change of Heart*.**

a) How are the people feeling, do you think? What are they talking about?

b) Now read this scene from the play and check your answers. Does anyone in the class have the same problem?

Act 1, Scene 2

an autumn evening in the Baileys' kitchen

MR BAILEY	(*to Andy*) We had a nice chat to your teachers at the parents' meeting this evening.
ANDY	Actually, dad, I've been meaning to talk to you about that.
MR BAILEY	Were you worried? Well, you needn't have been. Your teachers are very happy with your work. In fact, we didn't have to stay at the meeting very long. They all had only one thing to say: you're doing brilliantly.
MRS BAILEY	We're both proud of you! (*She's enjoying her meal.*)
ANDY	Thanks mum. Actually, I *was* a bit worried but not about my grades. (*playing with his food*) I . . .
MR BAILEY	You'd better start thinking about what university you want to go to. With your expected grades, you'll have a choice!
ANDY	Well, that's what I want to talk to you about. I don't want to go to university.
MRS BAILEY	You *what*? (*putting down her knife and fork quickly*) Oh, of course, it's the money. You're worried about the money, aren't you? Well, let us worry about that. You needn't give it a second thought. Just concentrate on your studies and . . .
ANDY	Mum! You're not listening to me. I'm not going to university. I've got other plans.
MR BAILEY	What are you saying, Andy?
ANDY	I've thought about it very carefully and I've decided to leave school at the end of the year and become a football player.
MR BAILEY	(*standing up suddenly*) A football player! A bright lad like you!
MRS BAILEY	Oh, Andy! How can you do this to us? We've worked hard to give you a good education. You've got a brilliant future ahead of you. And now you tell us you want to be a football player!
ANDY	I'm sorry if you're disappointed. But, look, you needn't worry about me. I do have a brilliant future – as a football player.
MR BAILEY	You're right, Andy, we are disappointed. We don't need to tell you that. But listen. You've still got plenty of time. You don't have to make any decisions now. Why don't you think things over for a few days?
ANDY	OK, dad. But my mind's already made up.

Line numbers: 5, 10, 15, 20, 25, 30, 35, 40

10 **Mark these sentences True or False. Which lines in the text helped you decide?**

1 Andy was worried about his school results.
2 He is a good student.
3 Mr and Mrs Bailey knew their son wanted to become a football player.
4 Andy's parents react to his news in the same way.
5 Mr Bailey hopes Andy will change his mind.
6 Andy thinks he's very good at football.
7 Andy needs more time to think about his future.

Compare your answers with your partner.

Writing

⭐ *A summary is a short account giving the main points. When you write a summary:*

1 Read carefully through the text and mark the important points, leaving out the details.

2 Make notes about the information you have marked.

*3 Write short sentences using your notes and link them with words like **in addition, however, although** and **because**.*

11 Get ready to write a summary.

a) Read through the scene of the play. Mark the important points.

b) Make notes about the points you marked in a).

c) Expand your notes into sentences.
    EXAMPLE: *Andy Bailey is a good student and both his teachers and his parents are happy with his work.*

d) Compare summaries with your partner.

Grammar

Absence of obligation

1 Present

a) Speaker's authority or advice
Andy's mum doesn't think it's necessary for Andy to worry about the money to pay for his studies.

Mrs Bailey: You **needn't give** it a second thought. (*now or in the future*)

b) External authority or circumstances
There is plenty of time for Andy to make up his mind. It isn't necessary for him to decide now.

Mr Bailey: You **don't** **have** **need** to **make** any decisions now.

2 Past

a) *It wasn't necessary to worry because everything was fine – but Andy worried anyway.*

Mr Bailey: You **needn't have been** worried.

b) *It wasn't necessary for Andy's parents to stay at the meeting very long, so they didn't.*

Mr Bailey: We **didn't** **have** **need** to **stay** very long.

12 Read these sentences. Match them with the different points in the grammar box (1a–2b).

1 (*Teacher to student*) 'It isn't necessary to write two pages. One is enough.'
2 (*One student to another*) 'It isn't necessary to pay at the disco. It's free for students.'
3 (*Child to parent*) 'It wasn't necessary to get the bus today. Petra's mother drove us home.'
4 (*Parent to child*) 'I don't think it's necessary for you to work all day. A couple of hours is enough.'
5 (*Coach to player*) 'It wasn't necessary to get here an hour early. Two minutes would have been enough.'
6 (*Brother to sister*) 'Let's ask mum if we can watch the film tonight. Tomorrow's Saturday so it isn't necessary to get up early.'

13 Rewrite the sentences in Exercise 12 using *needn't, don't need to, don't have to, didn't have to, didn't need to* or *needn't have*.

EXAMPLE: 1 *You needn't write two pages. One is enough.*

Pronunciation

14 Get ready to be an actor!

a) Make groups of three. How do you feel? Make a short list of words which describe your feelings:
   Student A: You are Andy Bailey. Your parents are very proud of you and want you to go to university. You are going to disappoint them.
   Student B: You are Mr Bailey. You are very proud of your son and you want the best for him. Now he tells you he wants to be a football player.
   Student C: You are Mrs Bailey. You want the best for your son and have made sacrifices to give him a good education. Now your clever son tells you your dreams for him won't come true.

b) ☐ Read the scene as you listen to a recording of it. Mark the words which your character emphasises.

c) Practise reading your part emphasising the words you marked in b). Remember how you are feeling!

d) In your groups, read out the scene.

15 Get ready to discuss the scene from the play.

a) Choose the alternatives you agree with.
   1 Andy should go to university and forget about football.
   2 Andy should do what he wants: it's his life.
   3 Andy should go to university and play football after university if he wants.
   4 Mr and Mrs Bailey should make Andy give up football.
   5 Andy should go to university and play football in his spare time.
   6 Mr and Mrs Bailey should make Andy stay on at school and talk about his football career when he has taken his final exams.

b) Compare your answers in a) in groups. You must all agree.

Writing

16 In your groups, write the next scene of the play. Use your ideas from Exercise 15.

In the dead of the night

1 Label the pictures with words from the box.

dream	insomnia	sleep walk
have a nightmare	snore	

1

2

3

4

5

Do you ever dream, sleep walk, have nightmares, snore or suffer from insomnia? Ask your partner.

Reading

2 Mark these sentences True or False before reading the text.

1 We sleep only in order to rest from physical activity.
2 When we sleep, our brain is inactive.
3 Sleep helps us memorise things we have learnt during the day.
4 We can dream all night.
5 Animals dream too.

Read the text and check your answers. Were you right?

Sleeping like a baby

We do it. Animals do it. Even plants do it. Night after night we close our eyes and are 'dead to the world' for hours. Have you ever wondered why we sleep, and what happens to your body and your brain once you have shut your eyes? Thanks to research carried out
5 in sleep laboratories it is now possible to find out.

The sleep cycle has three different phases which are repeated through the night.

It is ten o'clock at night. Three-month-old Ian has just gone to sleep. Doctors have attached wires from his face and head to a
10 special machine in order to . . . . . . Despite . . . . . , Ian's body can react to his environment. If you touched his face gently, his hand would push yours away. Ian has entered a phase of his sleep cycle called *light sleep*.

It is now 10.30. Whereas a few minutes ago he would have
15 responded to gentle touching Ian now doesn't react to noise or any other minor disturbance. He has entered a new phase of sleep, *deep sleep*. Scientists used to think that the purpose of this phase was for the body to recover from physical activity. However, ... We now know that the main purpose of deep sleep is to give the brain a
20 rest from mental activity. For this reason, ... In addition, ... This makes deep sleep all the more important.

At 11.30, after another period of light sleep, Ian enters the final phase of the sleep cycle: *paradoxical sleep*. It is called 'paradoxical' because, on the one hand, our muscles are inactive
25 but, on the other hand, our brain is even more active than when we are awake. The rapid movements of our eyes show this intense mental activity. During this phase our brains memorise what we learnt when we were awake. So when you're revising for an exam,

70

Words and phrases like **for example**, **however** or **consequently** show the logical relationship between two sentences or two parts of a sentence. These connectors can help you predict what follows.

3 Can you guess what comes after the connectors in the text? Complete the sentences in the text with these phrases.

1 ... this has been proved wrong.
2 ... from the age of twelve we spend only 20 per cent of our sleep time in this phase.
3 ... record the activity of his brain during the night.
4 ... the substance which makes us grow is made during these periods of deep sleep.
5 ... deep sleep is essential for our good health and happiness.
6 ... the fact that he looks completely still, ...
7 ... they spend 60 per cent of their nights in paradoxical sleep.

Ian happy . . .

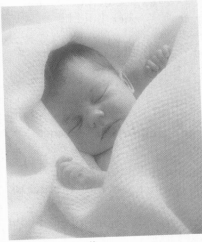

. . . and tranquil

remember to get plenty of
30 sleep. Otherwise you'll
forget what you learnt!
Babies have a lot to learn
and memorise. Consequently,
. . . . . whereas . . . . . .
35 Ian's face is showing lots
of different emotions. The
amazing thing is that at his
age he still can't show these
emotions when he is awake.
40 What is happening? Ian is
dreaming. Some people
believe that the real
meaning of a dream is
locked away in the back of
45 the dreamer's mind. In
people as well as in animals
dreaming occurs during
paradoxical sleep.
   If you are unlucky
50 enough to have insomnia
one night, watch other
members of your family
sleeping. Perhaps you can
guess what phase they are
55 in and from the expressions
on their faces you may even
guess what they are
dreaming!

4 Underline the connectors in the text and complete the sentences.

1 *In order to* introduces a purpose.
2 ____ introduces a reason.
3 ____ and ____ introduce a result.
4 *And*, ____ and ____ introduce a similar idea.
5 ____ . . . ____ introduces a comparison.
6 ____, ____ and ____ introduce a contrasting idea.

5 Match the sentences, then link them using *for this reason, in addition, on the other hand, because* and *whereas*.

1 If we don't sleep well at night, we feel tired the next morning.
2 Sometimes we can't remember our dreams.
3 Plants have to rest during the night.
4 Dolphins stay awake all the time.
5 On the one hand, a nap can make us feel fresh and alert.

a) They are thought to be one of the few mammals who don't dream.
b) We could have trouble remembering what we have learnt.
c) A long nap can stop us from sleeping well at night.
d) At other times we remember them very clearly.
e) They need sunlight for their chemical processes to happen.

Listening

When you want to make notes about information you hear, listen for the main points and then write down a few important words under each main point. Don't try to write whole sentences! Your notes will help you reconstruct the important information later.

6 🔊 **You're going to listen to a conversation.**

a) What is it about?

b) Listen again. Tick (✓) the things which are mentioned in the conversation and number them in the order they are first mentioned.
 • balls of fire • water • sun • river
 • what dreams tell us • flowers • walking

c) Listen again. Make notes about what the speakers say about the things you ticked in b). Then make sentences to give an idea of what the speakers said.
 EXAMPLE: *water: warm then cold, deep . . .*
 The water in the river was warm but then it got cold and deep . . .

Grammar

Expressing regret about the past

Wish (that) **+ Past Perfect**

She told her friend about her dream and now she is sorry.
 ⟶ **I wish I hadn't said** anything about it.

If only **+ Past Perfect**

In her dream she is sorry that she brought the balls of fire with her.
 ⟶ **If only I hadn't brought** these things with me.

Regret **+ verb-*ing***

In her dream she is sorry that she got into the river.
 ⟶ **I regret getting** into the river.

---

7 Rewrite the sentences to express regret.

EXAMPLE: 1 *He wishes he hadn't missed the horror film.*

1 My brother is really sorry he missed the horror film last night. He wishes . . .
2 I stayed up late last night. I regret it now. If only . . .
3 It was a bad idea to sleep on the floor! My back is really hurting! I regret . . .
4 Margaret left the window open and her desk got wet. It was silly of her! She wishes . . .
5 Why didn't you tell me about the exam? I didn't study for it. If only . . .
6 Jim's parents bought him an electric guitar. They regret it now! They regret . . .

8 Write a list of things you did recently and which you are now sorry about. Write sentences using *wish* + Past Perfect, *if only* and *regret*.

EXAMPLE: *My friends persuaded me to have my hair cut. I wish I hadn't listened to them. I don't like it short.*

Word watch

⭐ *Some verbs in English can be followed by -**ing** or by **to** + infinitive. The choice of -**ing** or **to** + infinitive changes the meaning of the verb:*
 I remembered to **shut** the door. *(I remembered first, then I shut the door.)*
 I remember **shutting** the door. *(Shutting is the first action and remember is the second.)*

---

9 Match the sentences on the left with the meanings on the right.

1 'I remember going into my parents' bed when I was little.'	a) I'm sorry I did that.
2 'I remembered to turn off the lights before going to bed.'	b) I'm sorry I now have to do this.
3 'I regret watching that film last night. It gave me nightmares!'	c) I remembered and then I did it.
4 'I regret to tell you that you have failed your exam.'	d) I have a memory of this past action.

10 Using *remember* or *regret*, write a sentence about something you:

1 have a memory of from childhood.
2 often forget to do but which you didn't forget to do recently.
3 are sorry you did to a friend or a member of your family.

Try to find someone who has at least two answers similar to yours.

Get talking

11 You are going to analyse some dreams.

a) Mark these expressions CA (complete agreement), PA (partial agreement) or CD (complete disagreement).
- 'Rubbish!'
- 'I don't agree at all.'
- 'Yes, but on the other hand . . .'
- 'Yes, I see what you mean but . . .'
- 'Jose has a point there.'
- 'That's right.'

b) Pair A: Turn to page 103.
   Pair B: Turn to page 106.

c) Pair A and B work together. Use your notes and interpret both dreams. Answer these questions and use the expressions in a).
   1 Julius Caesar dreamt he was flying. What do you think this meant?
   2 In Calpurnia's dream, what do you think the house collapsing meant?
   3 What do you think the black cat symbolised in Napoleon's dream?
   4 Do you think the dreams were premonitions or simply coincidence?

d) Tell the rest of the class your interpretation.

Pronunciation

12 Read the poem.

a) What makes the noises, do you think?

> Bully night
> I do not like
> the noises that you make
> The creaking and the shrieking
> that keep me
> fast awake.
>
> **from** *Bully Night* **by Roger McGough**

b) Find one word which rhymes with *fright* and two which rhyme with *take*.

c) 🖭 Mark the pauses at the end of each group of words which you would read continuously (tone groups). Listen and check your answers.

d) Practise reading the poem.

---

1 **What happened in Episode Five?**
2 **Read Episode Six and answer these questions.**
1 Why do Anya and Stefan think the police think they are weird?
2 What do Orpheus and the dragon represent?
3 What present does Anya's father give her and Stefan?

Vision of Danger

🖭 EPISODE SIX

Hot tears of frustration and humiliation stung Anya's eyes. 'They didn't believe us, mum. Even the police think we're just two
5 hysterical fans,' she sobbed.
   'What happened?' her father asked Stefan.
   'We went to the police to explain our suspicions,' said Stefan. 'They
10 just laughed at our story and said we were talking rubbish. Anya's right, they think we're just weird,' he said angrily.
   'Well I believe you,' said Anya's
15 father. 'I know how special you both are. You know that song you told me about? I think I may be able to help explain the words.'
   'Later, Edward,' warned Anya's
20 mother. 'They need to rest now.'
   The following morning, Anya's

father showed Stefan and Anya the notes he'd been making.
   'Orpheus was a wonderful
25 musician. His singing was so amazing that rivers flowed upwards to hear him sing. But Orpheus is also a powerful symbol. In simple terms, he represents goodness and the
30 power of the spirit to solve conflicts.'
   'What about the dragon?' Anya asked anxiously. 'What does that mean?'
35 'It probably represents an obstacle. Or evil, a threat,' he explained.
   'So, what's the connection with Stone?' asked Stefan. 'We know
40 he's a wonderful musician but – '
   'Maybe there isn't a connection at all. You can't be sure your feelings have anything to do with this singer.'
45 Anya sighed with relief. 'Thanks dad. I feel better already.

But we'd still like to go to the concert tomorrow night.'
   'And you will. Here are the
50 tickets,' said her father. 'Enjoy yourselves!'

3 **Think about the words of the song Anya and Stefan keep hearing. What do you think the danger to Stone is?**
4 **Do you think Anya and Stefan will enjoy the concert? Why (not)?**

Revision

Reading

1 Read the extracts from the reviews of a book. Answer the questions.

1 Which phrases tell you the critics' attitude?

2 Where did the reviews first appear?

3 What 'strangest' and 'most disturbing experience' is the book about, do you think?

Read the review below and check your answer to Question 3.

'A sympathetically written and extraordinarily interesting account of one of the strangest and most disturbing experiences a modern woman ever lived through.' Peter Quennell, *Daily Mail*

'A story brilliantly told.' *Observer*

'What a wonderful book! Now that I have finished it, I want to read it again.' John Betjeman, *Daily Herald*

'I can't understand what they're talking about!'
by Patricia Fontanell

Monica Baldwin: I LEAP OVER THE WALL
Hamish Hamilton £4.95

Monica sat without moving, her tongue sticking to the roof of her mouth, her eyes popping out of her head. She was overwhelmed by shock. She had never imagined 'such lurid colours, undreamed-of
5 situations, or amazing technique'. On the screen, Donald Duck ran around, telling his nephews off. Everybody in the cinema was laughing, they were obviously enjoying the cartoon. Monica had never seen a Disney film before, or a talking film, for that
10 matter.

In 1914, twenty-eight years before, she had gone into a small isolated religious community. She had only recently left. At first she was very excited because of . . . . . . (1), but soon she started having
15 difficulties. Everyday life as she had known it had been radically changed by technological developments.

She found World War II London to be a bewildering world where the car had replaced the
20 horse and carriage. Women wore short skirts and makeup, and a lot of them worked because the men were away fighting. It was all a bit of a shock for Monica. Her sister promptly gave her a pair of stockings – she needn't have done. 'I can't possibly
25 go out in these!' she exclaimed in horror. 'They make my legs look naked.' Whereas . . . . . . (2), her sister had given her a pair of the new skin-coloured transparent ones.

However, ... (3), it was the fact that the
30 English language had changed so much! Some people listened to the 'radio' – it took her some time to work out they were using the American word for what to her was a 'wireless'. When friends talked excitedly about 'jazz', she could only say that she
35 had never heard of this 'new' form of music. In addition, ... (4). What did people mean when they said 'Believe it or not'?

Monica enjoyed going to the new 'cafeterias' and restaurants, provided somebody explained the menu
40 to her. Otherwise she just couldn't make sense of the list of dishes. She tried reading newspapers in order to . . . . . . (5), but they only made her feel stupid. They talked about 'Hollywood' and 'robots', which she wasn't familiar with. She probably wished she
45 hadn't ever left the community.

Despite the difficulties, ... (6) and in 1949 she published *I Leap Over the Wall*, a moving and amusing account of her arrival in a new and puzzling world, which spoke a different language. Her story
50 is a dramatic illustration of the fact that language is not static. Written in a simple but lively prose, the book helps us understand how language
55 is constantly changing to reflect an ever-changing world. These days, if somebody had spent thirty years on a desert island,
60 how many words and expressions would be new to them?

2 **Read the review again. Choose the correct alternative to complete each sentence.**

1 her happiness/her return to the outside world
2 she liked the modern transparent silk stockings/she was used to old-fashioned thick stockings
3 clothes puzzled Monica the most/it was not what Monica saw that puzzled her the most
4 there were many new expressions/many expressions had not changed
5 catch up with the world/try reading books
6 she went back/she didn't go back

3 **Find out what these words refer to.**

1 they (1.07)
2 it (1.15)
3 It (1.22)
4 these (1.25)
5 they (1.37)
6 they (1.42)
7 them (1.62) (used to avoid the longer him/her)

4 **Answer the questions.**

1 Why was Monica so shocked when she saw the Donald Duck cartoon?
2 What surprised her about the appearance and activities of women? Why?
3 Why do you think the terms 'Hollywood' and 'robots' were new to Monica?
4 How does Patricia Fontanell feel about the book? Which phrases tell you?
5 Monica was forty-nine when she returned to the outside world. Do you think she did the right thing? Why (not)?

5 **In pairs, write a paragraph describing Monica.**

a) Write about what you imagine her general appearance and character are like.
b) Compare your paragraph with another pair's.

6 **If you had been on a desert island for the past eight years, what things, customs and words would most surprise you when you returned home? Discuss this with your partner and then write six sentences.**

EXAMPLE: *If I had been on a desert island for eight years, I would find the Internet amazing.*

The wider world

7 **New words and expressions are constantly appearing in the English language. As more people start using them they are put into dictionaries and become part of the language.**

a) Can you think of three words in your language which didn't exist when you were eight years old?
b) Are they in the dictionary?

Listening

8 ▭ **Listen to extracts from three conversations. Answer the questions.**

a) What is the topic in each case?
b) How do you think each conversation started? Write one or two questions the first speaker was probably asked before you started listening.

Project

9 **In groups, find out how much your language has changed.**

a) Each member of the group talks to three older people, your grandmother for example, in your own language. Ask them:
　1 if they can think of three words or expressions that were not used when they were young.
　2 if they know of any words that have changed their meaning.
　3 what they think about changes in the language.
b) In English (except for the actual words, of course!) make notes about what you are going to report to the rest of the group.
c) Exchange information in your group. Can you explain your findings?
d) Prepare a poster about the way your language has changed.
　1 Decide which of the new words/meanings to include.
　2 Decide which of the opinions to include. Aim for a balance of positive and negative. Include the group's opinions as well.

Grammar practice

1 **It's almost the beginning of the new academic year. Look at the school calendar and complete the sentences in the dialogue with the Present Simple or Present Continuous of the verbs in brackets. (Unit 13)**

```
Autumn term:  4 Sept-9 Dec
Half term:    16-20 Oct
Exams:        28 Nov-2 Dec
```

LUCY: Look, the school calendar arrived today.

MEG: Oh, yes? When ____ (1 classes, start)?

LUCY: On September 4th. That's early!

MEG: A lot earlier than I thought! We ____ (2 not come back) from holiday till the 6th!

LUCY: Lucky you. You'll miss a couple of days.

MEG: And when ____ (3 term, end)?

LUCY: On December 9th. The end of term exams ____ (4 be) from 28th November to 2nd December.

MEG: Oh, so term ____ (5 finish) early! Good, we ____ (6 visit) my gran in Australia then.

LUCY: You're always going away to exciting places! The only place I ____ (7 go) to this year is Devon – camping in October.

MEG: That sounds good, don't complain. And you'll miss school!

LUCY: No such luck. We ____ (8 go) on the 16th, when we ____ (9 be) on half term holiday.

2 **Complete the sentences with the Present Simple or Present Continuous of the verbs in the box. Careful: one verb is used twice. (Unit 13)**

```
love  have got  smell  have  wish  not mind  think
```

Dear Natalie,

I ____ a great time at my cousins'. They ____ a small boat and we go fishing every evening. The sea is beautiful – I ____ it! Tonight we caught a bucket full of fish. As I sit here writing to you the whole house ____ of it! But I ____ at all. In fact, I quite like it. We ____ of going up into the mountains tomorrow. Mario ____ there's a ruined castle up there, so we're going to look for it.

____ you were here. Love,

Sophie

3 **Write conditional sentences using the words in brackets. (Unit 14)**

1 Modelling can be a good career but don't expect it to last forever. (as long as)

2 You won't still be a successful model at thirty if you're not extremely good looking. (unless)

3 It is easy to reconstruct pre-Colombian towns, but only if you have a computer. (provided that)

4 You can become a TV addict if you don't limit your viewing time to a few programmes a day. (unless)

5 In the TV programme, the Gladiators' contenders can win, but they have to be very fit and very, very fast. (as long as)

6 The beaches will continue to be clean but only if people always put their rubbish in the bins. (providing)

4 **Write conditional sentences about Peru's Nazca mystery. (Unit 14)**

EXAMPLE: 1 *If the pilots flying over Peru's Nazca desert hadn't observed strange patterns on the ground, the world wouldn't know about the Nazca figures.*

1 Pilots flying over southern Peru's Nazca desert observed strange patterns on the ground. That is how the world knows about the Nazca figures.

2 The Nazcans weren't able to fly. That is why the gigantic figures drawn on the earth are so amazing.

3 Archeologist Maria Reiche worked tirelessly, she never gave up. As a result, we have got many photographs and detailed maps of the figures.

4 She wrote *Mystery on the Desert*. That is how we know about her work.

5 The Nazcans had a knowledge of arithmetic. That is why the lines are so precise.

6 Whole generations of Nazcans worked on the desert markings, so the figures are complex and mysterious.

5 **Unscramble the sentences. (Unit 15)**

1 had/Bob/shirt/old/put/scruffy/a/on

2 wearing/Nancy/long/dress/beautiful/silk/a/was

3 together/walking/street/twisting/along/narrow/they/were/the

4 met/old/they/mysterious/man/a

5 afraid/him/of/were/they

6 thought/dangerous/a/they/he/lunatic/was

7 them/was/he/afraid/of

8 thought/were/they/he/punks!/violent/nasty

6 Match the phrasal verbs with the correct definitions. Fill in the blanks in the example sentences with the correct form of the verb. (Unit 15)

> take off make up give up

1 *v. to invent a story or piece of information to deceive people.* They later discovered it wasn't true, she ____ the whole thing.
2 *v. to admit you cannot do something and stop trying.* I'm determined to solve the puzzle. I don't want to just ____.
3 *v. to rise into the air.* The plane ____ on time.
4 *v. to become friends again after a quarrel.* We have many quarrels, but we soon ____ afterwards.
5 *v. to stop having or doing something.* Selma hated her job, so she ____ it ____.
6 *v. to remove.* Alice came in and ____ her jacket.

7 Express regret about these situations and examples of people's behaviour. Use *I wish , if only* or *I regret*. (Units 16 and 17)

1 You are in the middle of your final exams and the next door neighbour insists on playing the stereo at top volume.
2 You were very rude to your mother.
3 More people become homeless every day.
4 Some of your friends drop rubbish in the street.
5 Your parents worry too much about your future.
6 You agreed to take Sam (the next door neighbour's dog) for a walk every day.
7 It is dangerous to walk in some areas of big cities.
8 Your English teacher has asked you to read the whole of *Jane Eyre* for next Monday.

8 What would you say in these situations? Use *need*. (Unit 16)

1 You don't think it's necessary for your mother to make your breakfast every day.
2 It wasn't necessary for you to finish reading the book for today, so you watched television instead.
3 It wasn't necessary for Gaby to wash the jumper you'd lent her, but she did anyway.
4 It isn't necessary to wear a uniform at your school.
5 It was not necessary of Mrs Tibbit to bring you a present. It was very kind of her to do so.
6 It isn't necessary for your father to get up early to take you to school. There are no classes tomorrow.

Grammar

1 talk about future plans and arrangements using the Present Simple. (Unit 13)
2 use verbs of feelings, perception, mental activity and possession in the correct form. (Unit 13)
3 express conditions using *unless, provided/providing (that)* and *as long as.* (Unit 14)
4 talk about imagined conditions in the past and their past and present consequences (Third and Mixed Conditionals). (Unit 14)
5 use adjectives in the correct order. (Unit 15)
6 use phrasal verbs which function with and without an object. (Unit 15)
7 express unhappiness about situations and people's behaviour using *wish + would/*Past Simple. (Unit 16)
8 talk about absence of obligation using *needn't, don't/didn't have to/need to* and *needn't have.* (Unit 16)
9 express regret about the past using *wish (that) +* Past Perfect, *if only* + Past Perfect and *regret +* verb–*ing.* (Unit 17)

Skills

READING

- identify the author's opinion in a review. (Unit 13)
- understand a text better by identifying words which avoid repetition. (Unit 14)
- predict what follows from the connectors used. (Unit 17)

WRITING

- describe people's general appearance and character. (Unit 15)
- write summaries. (Unit 16)

LISTENING

- understand a conversation that has already started by guessing the topic and making deductions. (Unit 14)
- take notes efficiently. (Unit 17)

SPEAKING

- ask for, make and react to suggestions. (Unit 13)
- express degrees of (dis)agreement. (Unit 17)

How was it done?

1 Answer the questions.

1 What are these machines called?
2 Have you got one? Have many of your friends got one?
3 Do you think it is a good invention? Why (not)?
4 Do you know how these machines were invented?

Reading

2 Scan the text and check or find out the answer to question 4 in Exercise 1.

3 Read the text and complete the notes on it.

Walkman
Creator: Akio Morita –   Sony . . . . . .
                            keen golfer
                            . . . . . .

Idea: . . . . . ., portable, stereo music player
Before that: Pressman –   redesigned by . . . . . .
                           sound ——> . . . . . .

General Sony opinion:
no sales –   couldn't record
                           . . . . . .

Launched: July, ...
Improvement within 4 years: . . . . . .
Version with play/record function: . . . . . .
Result: . . . . . . sold worldwide

Music on the move

A keen golfer and lover of music, Sony chief executive Akio Morita wanted a lightweight machine that would play cassettes and could be taken everywhere. It had to have stereo
5 sound, and the hi-fi components had to be made small and light enough for it to be carried around easily.

The electronics engineering team at Sony redesigned a small portable tape recorder
10 called the 'Pressman' so that it gave out stereo sound. However, they were dismayed that they were not able to produce a small model that would record.

It was widely believed within Sony that the
15 personal stereo wouldn't sell. Apart from its inability to record, it was thought that users would find the headphones annoying.

Despite these reservations, Morita continued to believe in the product. Without bothering to
20 conduct the usual market research, he gave the go-ahead and the first Walkman was put on the market in July, 1979. For the first twelve months it had no competition. Sony's competitors thought the Walkman might be a
25 commercial failure.

By the time the competitors realised that the product was selling, Sony had been busy making improvements which ensured that they would always stay one step ahead.
30 Within four years, the Walkman had been reduced to half its original size. The range of products now includes water-resistant sports models, brightly coloured children's Walkmans and even a Video Walkman. In its
35 short history more than 100 million Walkmans have been sold worldwide.

Sony have also taught the CD how to walk: they have a Discman and a MiniDisc Walkman which also records. Morita's music on the
40 move has become entertainment on the move – and not only for golfers!

Grammar

> **Passive voice**
>
> **1** Suitable form of *be* + **past participle** of a **transitive verb.**
>
> The Walkman **could be taken** everywhere.
> *People **could take** the Walkman everywhere.*
>
> The components **had to be made** small enough . . .
> *They **had to make** the components small enough . . .*
>
> More than 100 million Walkmans **have been sold** worldwide.
> *Shops worldwide **have sold** more than 100 million Walkmans.*
>
> **2** **Impersonal** *it* + suitable form of *be* + **past participle** of a **reporting verb** e.g. *think, say, believe.*
> *Refers to the opinion of people in general or of an unspecified group of people.*
>
> **It was** widely **believed** it wouldn't sell.
> *People in general thought this.*

4 **Fill in the blanks with the correct form of the verb in brackets (Passive or Active), or with the impersonal *it* and the verb given.**

1 When wristwatches first ____ (appear) at around the turn of the century, ____ (people in general – think) they were ridiculous. Less resistant to shock and humidity than the old chain watches, they ____ (consider) wholly unreliable. ____ (people in general – believe) they had little future.
2 During the Napoleonic wars, the French ____ (need) to feed their army. Napoleon offered a prize of 12,000 francs for a solution. That is when the tin can ____ (invent).
  Tin cans ____ (send) to the battlefield. But the problem was then how to open them. This proved very difficult. Many of Napoleon's soldiers ____ (go) into battle with only nine fingers! This went on for some time until finally the tin opener ____ (invent).
3 The first waterproof watch, the Rolex Oyster, ____ (make) by the Rolex company of Geneva. To test the first batch of watches, they ____ (immerse) in water for three weeks. ____ (people in general – think) the time-keeping would be affected but it did not show the slightest variation.

Vocabulary

5 **Fill in the gaps with the words in the box.**

> portable reliable improvements annoying
> tin opener headphones

1 Wristwatches nowadays are almost the same as when they were first invented. Few ____ have been necessary.
2 I know I shouldn't get angry, but it's very ____ to be next to someone listening to a personal stereo. You can hear a constant sound coming out of the ____ .
3 Bob would like to have a small television. He would prefer a ____ one so he can take it to his room when he wants to play a video game.
4 My watch is not at all ____ . Sometimes it's slow and sometimes it's fast.
5 Have you seen the ____ ? I can't find it and I'd like to have some tuna for lunch.

6 **Get ready to play a guessing game! Get into groups.**

a) Think of three machines. Write the names on a piece of paper.
b) To guess the other people's machines, ask Yes/No questions.
EXAMPLE:
CRISTINA: *Is it a music machine?*
ANDRES: *Yes.*
CRISTINA: *Can it be played on the beach?*

Writing

> ⭐ *Reports and accounts of scientific processes, developments and experiments are usually written in the passive voice because what happened is usually more important than the agent who made it happen. The passive voice also sounds more impersonal and objective.*

7 Look at the notes about video games. Use them to write a short account of the development of video games. Use the **Walkman** text on page 78 as a model.

Video games
Creator: Nolan Bushnell – engineering student, keen 'Spacewar' player on college computer, co-founder of 'Atari', 1972
Idea: computer games on home TV
Before that: 'Pong' game played in video arcades – written + later adapted by Bushnell
General opinion: No sales – called 'Home Pong'!
Launched: 1974, immediate success
Improvements since: More advanced games
Result: Many companies, e.g. Sega, Mario Brothers
Video games in 30%+ of US homes – not only children, parents too

---

8 Look at the picture on this page. Can you explain how this game is played?

1 How do you win the game?
2 Where do the players put their tokens at the beginning?
3 What are the dice for?
4 Why do players buy properties?
5 How do you use the houses and hotels?

Turn to page 103 and check your ideas against the instructions for the game.

Turn to page 103

Listening

> ⭐ *The brain works faster than a person can talk. When you listen to a talk, use this 'extra' time to think about what is being said and ask yourself what is going to follow. If you do this, you will find the talk easier to understand.*

9 📼 Listen to Charles, a Welsh boy, giving a talk on the history of Monopoly. When your teacher stops the tape, be prepared to make a comment about what is being said and/or to ask a question about what you think is going to follow.

10 📼 Listen again. Complete the sentences.

1 The first version of the game was called *Landlord's game*.
2 The 'Landlord's Game' was redesigned by . . .
3 At first, Monopoly was turned down by . . .
4 The first 5,000 copies were sold for . . .
5 The game of Monopoly has been translated . . .
6 In the translations, the streets are given . . .

Get talking

11 What makes a good talk?

a) Make a list of things that are important to you.
b) Compare your list with the one below.

> ⭐ *When you have to give a talk, remember what makes a good talk:*
> *1 An interesting topic*
> *2 A well-prepared presentation*
> *3 A speaker who speaks clearly, doesn't read but uses prompt cards, includes some humour, uses visuals, invites questions and answers them well*

---

c) 📼 Listen to Charles's talk again. On a scale of 1–4 (1=very good, 2=good, 3=OK, 4=poor) give a score to those elements of his talk which you can judge from listening to the cassette.
d) In groups, compare your scores. If they are different, explain why you gave them.

Pronunciation

12 🔲 **Listen to three mini-dialogues.**

a) Which is the most important stressed syllable in each answer?

1 What do you think of Monopoly?
  It was a remarkably good idea.
2 Are you sure?
  Yes, it was a remarkably good idea.
3 Don't you think it's too complicated?
  No, it was a remarkably good idea.

b) Why are *different* syllables the most important stressed syllables in each answer?

c) Practise saying the three mini-dialogues.

13 **Prepare a talk on a game or invention which you find interesting.**

a) Say what you're going to talk about and why you chose the topic.

b) Pick out the main features of the game or invention and deal with each one in turn.

c) Round off your talk by giving a personal view.

Be ready to give your talk and be judged by your classmates.

---

1 **Where are Anya and Stefan going? Who made this possible? Are Anya and Stefan still worried about Stone?**

2 **Read Episode Seven and make notes about:**

1 the equipment at the concert.
2 the rumours about Stone's career.
3 Stone's performance.
4 what happens on the stage halfway through the show.

Vision of Danger

🔲 EPISODE SEVEN

The underground train to Wembley was packed. It was obvious that everyone was going to Stone's concert at Wembley Stadium.
5 This might be the last time they would see their idol. There were rumours that Stone was retiring. But at that moment, nobody was contemplating that awful possibility.
10 As they came out of the station Anya and Stefan could see Wembley Stadium, shining like a gigantic diamond in the distance. When they reached the stadium, they gasped at
15 the sight of the huge stage and sound towers. Video screens, as tall as buildings, flanked the stage. The atmosphere was electrifying and, as the time for the show drew nearer,
20 the crowd started clapping rhythmically, demanding to see Stone.
Then the musicians came on stage and started to tune their instruments, much to the delight of the fans. It
25 wouldn't be long before Stone was on stage. Suddenly, all the lights went out. Amid a cloud of smoke and coloured lights, Stone appeared on the stage. The crowd went wild.
30 He knew how to please his audience. He sang all his best songs, making each person feel he was

singing just for them. Halfway through the show, he said he wanted
35 to make an important announcement.
It was at this point that Stefan got up, without warning, and started to push his way towards the stage. He
40 ignored the protests of the people he pushed out of his way and kept

looking at the far end of the stage.
'Stop him! Stop him!' he shouted.
Anya turned to see what Stefan
45 was looking at and, horrified, saw a man jump onto the stage, a gun in his hand. On the video screen, Anya, along with everybody else, watched the man fire and a body fall heavily
50 to the floor.

3 **'Anya watched the man fire and a body fall heavily to the floor.' Who do you think it was? What will happen to Stone? What will happen to Anya and Stefan?**

Young people in the news

1 Look at the photograph and at the newspaper headlines. Why is Peter in the news?

Runaway boy returns to reality after fantasy trip

Runaway boy is back home – but for how long?

Reading

2 Skim the two reports and check your answers to Exercise 1.

Peter Kerry on his return from Malaysia.

1

Peter Kerry, the 14-year-old who fulfilled his fantasy by running away to the Far East,
5 arrived back in Britain yesterday morning. Confronted by sixty photographers and journalists, Peter
10 looked unhappy and said he had no idea what the fuss was about. 'I have wanted to go to Malaysia for
15 quite a while. I was interested to see what it would be like. It's a nice country, and an interesting one at that.'
20 Peter, who seems perhaps to be at odds with his parents, ran away last Tuesday following an argument
25 over a can of spilt spaghetti and travelled by plane to Kuala Lumpur.
At first, everything
30 went well for Peter. He evaded security at Heathrow and Kuala Lumpur: the officers on duty at both airports
35 failed to notice that he was using his father's passport and that he had changed the photo. Later, however, he got
40 into difficulty when a hotel refused to accept the credit card belonging to his father. He then tried but failed
45 to cross the border into Singapore and instead travelled north. He was eventually spotted near the border with
50 Thailand. After being caught, the Malaysian authorities allowed him to leave the country on 'humanitar-
55 ian grounds'.
His father, John Kerry, said he hoped that in the end Peter 'could be cured of his
60 wanderlust'.

2

There was no hero's
35 welcome when two uniformed police officers in an old blue car
5 delivered Peter Kerry to his doorstep yesterday
40 morning.
His Malaysian escapade, made possible by his
10 father's passport and credit cards, came to a sad end as the officers took
45 his dirty old backpack out of the car and escorted
15 him to his front door. He had gone off to Malaysia
50 last Tuesday out of the blue after a disagreement over a spilt plate of
20 spaghetti.
If he felt any happiness at
55 being home, the 14-year-old didn't show it at all. He coolly said that if he
25 had not been caught trying to cross the Thai-
60 Malaysian border, he would have used his return ticket seven days
30 later.
Peter looked unrepentant. By and large things had gone well for him. He said little and spoke in a
35 low voice. He said that Malaysia was 'nice'. He had wanted to go there for 'quite a while'. When his mother kissed him on
40 the cheek, he froze.
Peter seems to be totally out of his parents' control. Mrs Kerry, his mother, later said that Peter was
45 quite a difficult boy and suggested his picture should be distributed by fax to every port and airport in the country.
50 That way people would recognise him and it would be impossible for him to 'do this again'. Her husband, asked how
55 much Peter's 14,000 mile trip would cost in all, replied, 'I've no idea and I dread to think.'
Peter is expected back at
60 school before the week is out and fellow students in Year Nine have been warned not to glamorise his travels.

3 Read the reports again and answer the questions.

1 Where did Peter go?
2 How did he pay for the trip?
3 How did he manage to get out of Britain and into Malaysia?
4 Where was he caught?
5 Why did he run away?

> Different newspapers have different ways of looking at the world. Some are more conservative and some more liberal. This affects the way they report the news: they each highlight different parts of a story and describe them in different ways. When you read a newspaper, try to identify its general outlook.

4 Read the reports again.

1 Match them with the correct headline.
2 On a scale of 1–5 (1=strong approval, 5=strong disapproval) how would you rate each paper's opinion of Peter's behaviour? Which words and phrases helped you decide?
EXAMPLE: *no hero's welcome* vs *Peter . . . arrived back in Britain.*

Get talking

> When you take part in a discussion:
> • Support what you say with reasons or examples.
> • Listen to others. Don't interrupt them.
> • Involve those who are not taking part. Ask, 'What do you think?'

5 Is Peter Kerry a confused and unhappy boy? Is he irresponsible and dishonest? Or do you think he is none of these things? Will he be cured of his 'wanderlust'? What do you think?

a) Discuss in groups of four or five.
b) Use the opinions expressed in the discussion to write a 150-word composition called 'Peter's wanderlust'. Make sure you link your ideas with the appropriate connectors. Look at page 71 again.

Grammar

> ### Fixed phrases with prepositions
>
> **at** – Peter seems perhaps to be **at odds with** his parents. (*in disagreement with*)
> He didn't show it **at all**. (*in any way*)
> It's a nice country, and an interesting one **at that**. (*besides*)
>
> **by** – **By and large** things had gone well. (*on the whole*)
> Mrs Kerry suggested his picture should be sent **by fax**. (*using a fax*)
>
> **in** – How much will the 14,000 mile trip cost **in all**? (*as the total*)
> Peter spoke **in a low voice**. (*softly*)
> Perhaps Peter will be cured of his wanderlust **in the end**. (*after a lot of time*)
>
> **on** – The immigration officers **on duty** didn't notice the forgery. (*who were working at the time*)
> They let him leave the country **on** humanitarian **grounds**. (*for humanitarian reasons*)
>
> **out** – Peter seems to be totally **out of** his parents' **control**. (*They don't have the power to direct him.*)
> He had gone to Malaysia **out of the blue**. (*unexpectedly*)

6 Complete the sentences with the correct phrases from the grammar box above.

1 She spoke _____ , so I could not quite understand what she was saying.
2 The cold weather came on _____ . Nobody was expecting these low temperatures in summer.
3 The guard is _____ at the museum until 7.00 tonight.
4 She could send the timetable by post, but it's quicker _____ .
5 At first he didn't like me _____ . I could tell by the way he never smiled at me.
6 They spent £300 _____ . They bought lots of books and CDs.
7 They are asking for the prisoners to be freed _____ humanitarian _____ . It's not fair to keep them locked up.
8 The car went _____ and crashed into the fence.

Word watch

We can add a prefix to a word to form the opposite, or near opposite. Some of these prefixes are:

un- *unhappy, unrepentant*

in- *indirect, inefficient*

im- *(usually before 'm' or 'p')* *immoral, impossible*

il- *(usually before 'l')* *illegal, illogical*

ir- *(usually before 'r')* *irregular, irresponsible*

dis- *disagree, disapprove, dishonest*

7 Fill in the blanks with the *opposite* of the words in the box.

efficient	happy	approve
possible	legal	responsible

1 Peter's mother is very ____ about her son's behaviour.
2 The police are questioning Peter because it is ____ to alter passports.
3 Interpol were not at all ____ . They found Peter quickly and without much information.
4 It is very difficult, almost ____ , to imagine a fourteen-year-old travelling alone like that.
5 Some people think it is ____ of parents not to control their children.
6 One of the newspapers obviously ____ of Peter's behaviour.

Schoolgirl wins fifth Golf World Championship

She is only twelve years old, but she has already been Junior Golf World Champion five times. The youngest golf player to have won five consecutive times, she has made it into the *Guinness Book of Records* too.

Lorena Ochoa, from Guadalajara, Mexico, started playing golf when she was three. 'Our house is in the local Country Club grounds, so my dad used to take me for short playing sessions when I was three. I had these little golf sticks,' she says. 'And she hit the ball well right from the beginning,' adds her proud father.

'When Lorena qualified for her first Junior Golf World Championship at the age of eight, I had doubts about taking her to San Diego to play in it. I was afraid the pressure would be too much for her or that she would be too upset if she didn't win,' he recalls. It was the president of the local golf association who persuaded him.

'I was so nervous that I couldn't go to the course on the day,' he confesses. Lorena, on the other hand, was as cool as a cucumber! 'It was as though she'd played there all her life. Quite amazing,' Mr Ochoa continues.

Lorena returned from San Diego with her first World Champion trophy. She's won another four since then. How does she do it? 'When I get to the course, I just start hitting balls and I concentrate. Then I watch my opponent,' explains Lorena. 'The most important thing in golf is concentration, and then relaxation.' According to some golfers the most frustrating thing is when you hit a ball 220 metres and it almost gets to the flag – and then it stops dead two metres away. It might take another five hits to get it in the hole. It's as if it didn't want to go in.

In spite of the odd frustrating moment Lorena loves the game and all the travelling when she takes part in championships. She would like to win a scholarship to a golfing school in the States. 'Then I could do the rounds as a pro.' Many would say she already plays like a pro.

8 Look at the photograph of Lorena in the Golf World Championship article on page 84. How similar to or different from Peter would you say she is?

Reading

9 🖭 Read the article. Then listen to the questions and write the answer after each one.

10 In pairs, answer these questions, then compare your answers with the rest of the class.

1 What do you think about Lorena's attitude to the game?
2 Do you think golf is making her miss out on activities which are normal for her age?
3 Would you like to be a Junior World Champion of a sport? Why (not)?

Grammar

As, like, as . . . as, as if, as though

as + (pro)noun (= *in the job, function or role of*)

I could do the rounds **as a professional**.
She would be a professional by then.

like + (pro)noun (= *similar to*)

She already plays **like a professional**.
Although she isn't one yet.

(as) + adjective + *as* + noun (= *definition by comparison*)

Lorena was **(as) cool as a cucumber**.
A cucumber is very cool. Lorena was very cool, not nervous at all.

as if/as though + a past tense
(= *unreal comparison*)

It was **as if/as though she had played** there all her life.
But she hasn't.

It is **as if/as though it didn't want** to go in.
But of course a ball can't decide not to go in.

She plays **as if/as though she was/were** a professional.
But she isn't one yet.

---

11 Fill in the blanks using *as* or *like*.

1 My aunt used to work ____ a nurse but she doesn't any more. She says she no longer has the energy to work ____ a dog!
2 I think she's completely mad, ____ nutty ____ a fruitcake!
3 Stop acting ____ a fool! This is serious.
4 Sally may look soft but she's ____ tough ____ nails.
5 At first, Lorena's father functioned ____ her coach. Later they hired a professional coach.
6 Jenny looks just ____ her mother.

12 Complete the sentences with an unreal comparison.

EXAMPLE: 1 *My parents sometimes treat me as if I were a child.*

1 My parents sometimes treat me as if . . .
2 Some teachers set homework as though . . .
3 Boys sometimes behave as if . . .
4 Girls sometimes act as though . . .
5 At times, I behave as if . . .

13 Role-play this situation in pairs. Develop it in any way you like.

Student A: You are Lorena Ochoa. You are flying to Tokyo for a golf tournament. You realise that the boy sitting next to you is Peter Kerry. You start talking to him.

Student B: You are Peter Kerry. You are travelling on a plane to Tokyo. You realise that the girl sitting next to you is Lorena Ochoa, Junior Golf World Champion. She starts talking to you.

Behind the scenes

1 **What are the names of Batman's partner, car, plane and biggest enemy?**

Reading

⭐ *Remember that the reason **why** you are reading determines the **way** you read. If you want to find a particular piece of information, like a name, without necessarily understanding the rest of the text, you can scan.*
If you want more specific information, you need to read more slowly and carefully.

2 **Scan the article and check your answers to Exercise 1.**

3 **Read the article again. Are these statements True or False?**

1 The film, which opened at the same time as many similar films, was a failure.
2 Before the film opened, fans were going to the cinema just to see the *Batman* advertisements.
3 The *Batman* set was the biggest one which had ever been made.
4 It was easy to film the Batwing as it crashed into Gotham Cathedral.
5 The car was difficult to handle. It had been made out of old car and plane parts.
6 Actor Michael Keaton would throw things about because he felt too hot in the rubber body suit.

'Good thinking, Batman'

The phrase, made famous by Batman's partner Robin, is sometimes used by 5 people to congratulate someone who has had a good idea. It could certainly be said to the producers of the film, 10 *Batman*.

Batman did amazingly well from the beginning. Despite having opened against strong 15 competition from *Indiana Jones and the Last Crusade, Star Trek V* and *Ghostbusters II, Batman* shot into the record books as the first film ever to gross $100,000,000 in ten days. Its huge success did not come as a surprise: cinema owners had 20 reported fans buying tickets for other films just to watch the ninety-second *Batman* promotion.

But it wasn't all plain sailing: the studio bosses had been very worried about the cost of the film. The set alone had cost more than $3,000,000. It was the second 25 biggest set ever made for a film.

Behind the scenes

Even with a mega set, models were often used as a supplement, for example when filming the Batwing scenes. The most complicated scene to film was the one 30 where the Batwing crashed into the steps of Gotham Cathedral. Four cameras were used at the same time.

The Batcar was a big problem too. Made out of two 1968 Chevrolet Impalas and bits of fighter aircraft, it was very difficult to control. It nearly ran a girl over, 35 and Batman kept getting his ears caught when the roof closed!

The Batman costume had its problems too. Some of the twenty-four Batman hoods were more comfortable than others, but none allowed actor Michael Keaton to 40 see sideways. In addition, they all made him partially deaf.

The body suits were like latex armour that simulated muscles. Feeling hot and bothered in all the rubber, Keaton would throw things about and kick furniture in 45 frustration. This in itself was a challenge: the cape he was wearing weighed 11 kg.

The face for Batman's arch enemy, The Joker, was made of synthetic pads moulded to actor Jack Nicholson's muscle 50 structure. It moved beautifully, like a second skin. But it was so white that it looked shapeless on film! 55 Makeup artists had to add shadowing effects.

So, was making the film a good idea? It certainly was. Not only 60 did the film and its sequels prove to be a huge commercial success, but Batman accessories became the thing for young people, and Prince's soundtrack *Who can you trust?* made number one.

Grammar

Participle clauses

Used mainly in written English to add information

1 Present Participle (*replaces active constructions*)
Examples:
a) Time
After expressions like while, when, before, after *and* since.
. . .when filming the Batwing scenes.
. . .when they filmed the Batwing scenes.

b) Reason
Feeling hot and bothered in all the rubber, Michael Keaton would throw things about.
He would throw things about because he was feeling hot and bothered.

2 Past Participle (*replaces mainly passive constructions*)
Examples:
a) Reason
Made out of bits of cars and aircraft, the Batcar was difficult to control.
Because it was made out of bits of cars and aircraft, the Batcar was difficult to control.

b) Relative clauses
It was one of the biggest sets **ever made.**
It was one of the biggest sets which had ever been made.

3 Perfect Participle (*replaces active constructions*)
Despite having opened against strong competition, *Batman* shot into the record books.
Opened *is the first action,* shot *is the second. Used for emphasis.*

4 Which of the concepts in the grammar box (1a-3) do these sentences illustrate?

1 On its opening day, *Batman Forever* made more money than any other film ever made.
2 Being totally white, the Joker's face didn't film well.
3 Made of rubber, the Batman costumes were very hot and uncomfortable.
4 Having worn the costumes in *Batman Forever*, actor Val Kilmer said lava would be preferable!

5 Rewrite the sentences using a participle clause instead of the words underlined.

EXAMPLE: 1 *Wanting the character to earn love, Spielberg made E.T. unattractive at first sight.*

1 Steven Spielberg made E.T. unattractive at first sight <u>because he wanted the character to earn love.</u>
2 Sylvester Stallone would sometimes fall asleep on his feet during the filming of *Rambo*. <u>The reason was that he was working a nineteen-hour day.</u>
3 In *Star Wars* an android <u>who is called R2D2</u> helps the hero.
4 <u>After he escapes</u> from the laboratory, Frankenstein sees his reflection in water.
5 The makers of *Robocop* mixed a cop movie with science fiction <u>because they wanted to play on people's fears of both technology and crime.</u>
6 <u>He travelled to the past in *Back to the Future*.</u> Michael J. Fox travelled to the future in *Back to the Future II*.
7 <u>Because it was made with the help of a computer programme,</u> the scenery in *First Knight* was easy to produce.

6 In pairs, ask and answer the questions.

1 Have you seen any of these films?
2 What were they about?
  - Superman IV
  - The Ninja Turtles
  - Cinderella
  - Casper
  - Dracula
  - The Flintstones
  - Jurassic Park
  - Addams Family Values

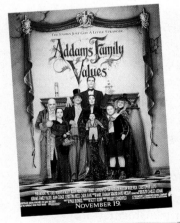

7 Which of the films in Exercise 6 (*Superman IV, Dracula, The Ninja Turtles, The Flintstones, Cinderella, Jurassic Park, Casper* and *Addams Family Values*) are mentioned in the book page opposite? Scan the text and find out.

8 Read the book page carefully and match the scenes with the special effects.

1 We can see Superman flying.	a) A puppeteer was manipulating the features by radio control.
2 We heard the floor collapse.	b) Sound engineers sawed a cabbage in half.
3 We saw enormous snow walkers carrying an army.	c) They used a wind machine and an optical printer.
4 The audience could see the Ninja Turtles smile.	d) They were pressing onto a pile of wood.
5 We hear the villain sawing an arm off a poor victim.	e) Mini models were filmed in stop motion.

Grammar

> **See/hear somebody do/doing something**
>
> **1** *Hear/see + object + infinitive*
> *We hear or see the **whole** of the action from beginning to end.*
> Crash! We **see** and **hear** the floor **collapse.**
>
> **2** *Hear/see + object + . . . -ing*
> *We hear or see **part** of the action, a few minutes (only).*
> We **saw** Superman **flying.**

9 In which of the films in Exercise 7 did these things happen? Write sentences using *see + object + . . . -ing* or infinitive.

EXAMPLE: 1 *In* Cinderella, *the audience sees . . .*

1 Fairy godmother turns a pumpkin into a carriage – audience sees the instant transformation.
2 Vampire sucks blood from his victims – audience sees part of the action.
3 Baby dinosaur breaks out of its eggshell – audience sees the whole process.
4 A paperboy delivers stone newspapers – audience sees part of his round.

What special effects do you think were used in item 3?

Special

Crash! We hear, and see, part of the building collapse. The heroine is left hanging by one hand onto a window ledge hundreds of metres
5 above the busy road. It looks as if she might fall to her death at any minute.
　Zoom! Along comes Superman, his cape flapping in the wind. He
10 takes hold of the girl and gently deposits her on firm ground.
　How do the film makers do it? The answer is special effects: the series of tricks and techniques used
15 to keep us glued to our seats.

High flyer

For us to see Superman flying, the actor has been filmed lying on his stomach in front of a brilliant blue screen. A wind machine makes
20 his hair and cape flap as if he were flying. The background scenes of the city are filmed separately from a low-flying aircraft. Later on, the two films are made into one by a machine called an optical printer so that Superman
25 appears to be flying over the city.

Mini models

Remember the battle scene from *The Empire Strikes Back* where we see towering snow walkers carrying the troops into battle?
30 Building life size snow walkers was impossible, so model makers created miniature versions. The models were then moved by stop motion: the camera filmed one frame at a time and the animators moved the
35 models between each frame.

effects

Animatronics

In films like *The Ninja Turtles,* the turtles
were actors in costumes. But the actors did
not control the turtles' facial expressions. The
40 expressions were created by a puppeteer who
moved the mouth, eyes and other features by
radio control. This is called 'animatronics'.

Cutting cabbage

Special effects are not only visual. A
45 collapsing floor may be suggested by a
recording of a real one, or by a pile of wood
which is pushed down from a height. Our
imagination also helps: if we hear a bang and
a woman scream, we might assume that
50 something terrible has happened to the
heroine.

If a suggestion is not enough and the real
thing cannot be recorded, sound engineers
will imitate the sound. When adults hear the
55 villain sawing somebody's arm off in a horror
film, sound engineers are really sawing a
cabbage in half. It is thought that the two
noises are similar!

Word watch

10 **Look at these words that are very similar.**

a) Match the words and the definitions.
  • shout • scream • wail

  1 cry out loudly on a high note in fear, pain or
  excitement
  2 cry out with a long sad sound suggesting
  sadness or pain
  3 say something very loudly

b) Listen to some sounds. Make notes about
what you hear.
EXAMPLE: *someone walking*

c) Compare your notes with your partner's. Do you
agree?
EXAMPLE:
ELA: *I heard someone walking.*
RAFAL: *Yes, and after that I heard . . .*
ELA: *I didn't hear that. I heard . . .*

Writing

> For a story to be clear to the reader, it should
> answer the following questions:
> 1 Who were the main characters?
> 2 What did the characters do? When? Where?
> Why? With whom?
> 3 What else happened?
> 4 How did the story end?
> If the story is complex, numbers 2 and 3 could be
> repeated several times.

11 **You're going to make up a story.**

a) In pairs, imagine a story to fit the sounds you
heard in Exercise 10b. Give the story an ending.

b) Write individual versions of the story. Make sure
the plot is clear to the reader.

c) Compare your version to your partner's. Is the
plot clear in both of them? Are your stories as a
whole different in any way?

Land of the brave?

Vocabulary

1 **Look at the adjectives in the box.**

cowardly	selfless	selfish	courageous
quick-witted	brave	cautious	foolhardy

a) Which one describes people who:
1 are able to control their fear?
2 care only about their own advantage, not other people?
3 take care to avoid risks?
4 think about other people, not themselves?
5 are courageous and ready to suffer danger or pain?
6 are afraid to face danger or pain?
7 take unwise risks?
8 are quick to understand things and act quickly?
EXAMPLE: 1 *courageous*

b) In your opinion, which of the adjectives in a) describe the people in the pictures below? Why?
EXAMPLE:
THORA: *The boy in picture one is quick-witted. He was reading but he acted quickly to save the little boy.*
KATERINA: *Yes, but perhaps someone told him to take care of the boy and he was reading instead, so he was being selfish.*

1

2

Reading

2 **Six sentences are missing from the newspaper report on page 91. Read the report and choose the correct sentence (a–f) to fill each gap (1–6). Say what punctuation and capital letters are missing.**

EXAMPLE: 1c *comma after 'pride' – this year's Children of Courage were the picture of modesty today – full stop*

a) I don't think I was brave
b) the cut was so bad that Mr McNestrie could not stop the bleeding
c) this year's Children of Courage were the picture of modesty today
d) another Child of Courage being honoured today was Abby Davis
e) at first she could hardly walk
f) I am very proud of him

3 **Read the report again. Who:**

1 has learnt to play football with a false foot?
2 did doctors think might not walk again?
3 rescued some children from a fire?
4 will probably be walking normally in 3–4 weeks?
5 bought clothes for ~~Romanian~~ orphans?
6 stopped his father's bleeding with a tea towel?

4 **Jon said, 'I don't think I was brave.' What do you think? Which of the adjectives in Exercise 1 would you apply to Jon, Abby, Carol, Lucy and Davy?**

3

posed by models

Bravest children have a nice line in modesty

While their parents glowed with pride . . . . . .(1) To hear a teenager describe how she managed to rescue three
5 small children from their burning home or a twelve-year-old explain how he was able to save his father's life, you would think they did it
10 every day.

Jon McNestrie's father owes his life to his son. Mr McNestrie severed a main artery while he was cleaning
15 a glass fish tank . . . . . .(2) Luckily for him, Jon managed to control it.
. . . . . .(3) said Jon. 'I did what anybody would have
20 done. I could see that my father was bleeding badly, so I grabbed a tea towel off the radiator and wrapped it tightly around his arm.'
25 Mr McNestrie was near death by the time he arrived at hospital and doctors believe Jon saved his life . . . . . .(4) He deserves this
30 award,' said Mr McNestrie.
. . . . . .(5) who is thirteen. Abby suffered huge injuries when she was run over by a

lorry two months ago. She
35 had multiple leg fractures and could not even stand up. Doctors feared she would never be able to walk again.

Showing incredible deter-
40 mination, Abby took her first steps only three and a half weeks after the accident . . . . . .(6) but she persevered. She has done so well that
45 doctors think she will be able to walk normally within less than a month. It won't be easy, but they are sure Abby will manage to do it.
50 Three other children were presented with their awards today. Carol Harris, aged fourteen, rescued three small children from their burning
55 home. 'I could hear them crying. I just had to get them out,' she said. Thirteen-year-old Lucy Karan looked after a group of ~~Romanian~~
60 orphans after raising money so she and her mother could buy clothes and take them to ~~Romania~~. And keen footballer Davy James,
65 fifteen, lost a foot in a bicycle accident but now plays with an artificial one.

All the Children of Courage were presented with
70 their awards by the Duchess of Kent at a ceremony in Westminster Abbey.

the ~~orphanage~~ orphanage.

Grammar

Ability: *could, be able to, manage to*

1 Future
Doctors think Abby **will be able to** walk normally within less than a month.

For particularly difficult actions:
She **will** probably **manage to** do it.

2 Past
a) Ability in general
Three and a half weeks later Abby **could** hardly walk/**was** hardly **able to** walk.

b) Ability on a specific occasion
Affirmative:
Lucy **was able to** raise money for ~~Romanian~~ orphans.
She was able to do this and she did it.

A teenager **managed to** rescue three children from their burning home.
She was able to do this difficult action and she did it.

Negative:
Mr McNestrie **couldn't/ wasn't able to/didn't manage to** stop the bleeding.

Before a verb of perception:
I **could** hear them crying.

5 **Complete the sentences using *could* whenever possible. If it is not possible, use a form of *be able to*.**

1 Lucy Karan's determination paid off. She ____ raise a lot of money for Romanian orphans.
2 Davy ____ ride a bike when he was five. He was good on roller skates too.
3 I ____ go to the ceremony next week.
4 Carol Harris ____ rescue the children by crawling into their room. She got an award for it.
5 Their grandfather ____ speak four languages and was learning a fifth one when he died.
6 The doctors ____ fit Davy with an artificial foot last year. He can even play football now.
7 The lorry driver ____ see that he was going to hit Abby, but he ____ (not) stop in time.

6 **Which of the above sentences can be completed with a form of *manage to*?**

7 **Write three sentences about your general abilities when you were ten. Write two sentences about things which you did only after a lot of effort.**

Pronunciation

8 🔲 **Listen to each of the dialogues being read twice.**

a) When does B indicate that he/she wants to be told more? Write 1 for the first reading and 2 for the second.
   1 A: Have you heard about the Children of Courage Awards?
      B: Yes.
   2 A: The awards were given out at a ceremony in Westminster Abbey.
      B: Uhmm.
   3 A: A boy got an award because he saved his father's life.
      B: Oh.
b) Does the intonation fall or rise when we want the speaker to continue? Does it rise or fall to signal the end of the conversation?
c) In pairs, take turns to practise the dialogues. Student B, use falling or rising intonation. Student A, tell your partner what the intonation meant to you.

Get talking

⭐ *When somebody is telling you something and you want to indicate that you are following and that you want the person to continue, you indicate it by a rising intonation or by using expressions like:*
What else?   And then?   Anything else?   Go on.

9 **Get into pairs. You are each going to look at three pictures which tell what happened to 15-year-old Louise when she was asked to baby-sit for her brother one evening. Take turns to describe them to your partner. Together, put the pictures in the correct order so that they tell Louise's story.**

Student A: Turn to page 102.
Student B: Turn to page 104.

Listening

10 🔲 **Listen to Louise tell the story.**

a) How similar was your version?

b) Listen again and complete the phrasal verbs with the correct particle.
   1 Louise had to stay ____.
   2 She thought her friends might laugh ____ her if she took Tom.
   3 Sally was surprised when Louise turned ____.
   4 She made ____ a story about her aunt.
   5 Tom waited for Louise to get ____.
   6 They ran ____ their parents when they were going to casualty.
   7 Louise's parents told her ____.

Grammar

Phrasal verbs

Type 1: intransitive verbs
verb + particle
Louise's parents were **going out.**
Also: get back, go back, stay in, turn up

Type 2: inseparable transitive verbs.
verb + particle + object
Louise didn't want to **look after Tom.**
Also: go through, laugh at, run into

Type 3: separable transitive verbs
verb + object + particle
She didn't want to **bring him/Tom along.**

If the object is a noun, it can also go after the particle, especially if it is very long.
verb + particle + object
She didn't want to **bring along her eight-year-old brother Tom.**

Also: make up, put on, tell off, turn down, turn off, turn on

---

Vision of Danger

🔊 EPISODE EIGHT

---

1 What would you like to happen in this last episode?
2 Read Episode Eight. Does it end as you would like it to?

Stefan lay very still in the middle of the stage. He had been shot while trying to disarm the man who had threatened Stone's life. Slowly, Anya made her way to the stage, not wanting to discover the worst. She bent down over Stefan and touched his face gently.

Stefan opened his eyes. 'Well, it looks like we did it!' he said smiling.

'Are you OK? You're bleeding!'

'It's only a graze, I think.' Stefan looked up. It was Stone! But all he had time to say was thank you before the security men took him quickly off stage. Anya and Stefan watched as police officers led the gunman away. He was a young man with long, messy hair. He looked as if he might burst into tears. His eyes met theirs for a brief moment.

'Not much of a dragon, is he?' said Stefan.

Stefan was sitting up in bed in hospital. Anya and her parents were sitting round him, all talking at the same time.

'Well, you two have become quite a couple of celebrities!' said Anya's mother. 'Just listen to what the papers say: "Knight in blue jeans kills the dragon".'

'"Young sleuths save Stone from rolling",' added Anya happily.

'It says here that the gunman was a strange and difficult man. He had lots of problems. Stone and his music put harmony into his life and solved his conflicts. So he hated the idea of Stone retiring,' said Anya's father. 'He hated the idea so much that he would have preferred to see him die.'

Everyone was shocked, and relieved that the gunman had failed.

'I'm going to miss all the attention when I go home,' Stefan laughed.

'I wish you didn't have to go so soon!' Anya complained.

'I'll be back. But promise me, no more mysteries to solve!'

Anya stood alone at the airport and watched the plane disappear into the sky. 'Bye, Stefan,' she whispered. 'We'll never really be apart. We both know that now.'

---

3 Why does Stefan say, 'Not much of a dragon, is he?' about the gunman?
4 What do the newspaper headlines mean?

---

11 Complete the sentences with the correct form of these phrasal verbs. The objects of the verbs are given in brackets. Put them in the correct place.

stay in	turn on	laugh at	go out
turn off	turn down	put on	get back
make up	tell off	look after	

1 Pete is too tired to ____ tonight, he would prefer to ____ and read a book.
2 They are real television addicts. They ____ (the television) when they get home from school and they only ____ (it) when it is time to go to bed. Their mother often ____ (them), but it doesn't make any difference.
3 When Paul ____ from his trip wearing that hat, everybody ____ (him). He looked so ridiculous!
4 Keira was in a hurry because she was going to ____ (the little boy next door) while his parents were out. She ____ (her long green coat) and left without saying goodbye.
5 He is such a liar! He ____ (these long and funny stories about UFOs).
6 I can't hear what you're saying, Karl. I'll go and ____ (the music), it's too loud.

12 You are going to play the phrasal verb game.

a) Choose a phrasal verb from Units 11, 15 or 22. Write it on a small piece of paper.
b) Fold the paper and give it to your teacher.
c) Pick a piece of paper. Can you make a correct sentence using the phrasal verb?

Let's keep talking

I **Why are you learning English? Write a list of as many reasons as you can think of.**

Read the article. Can you add to your list of reasons?

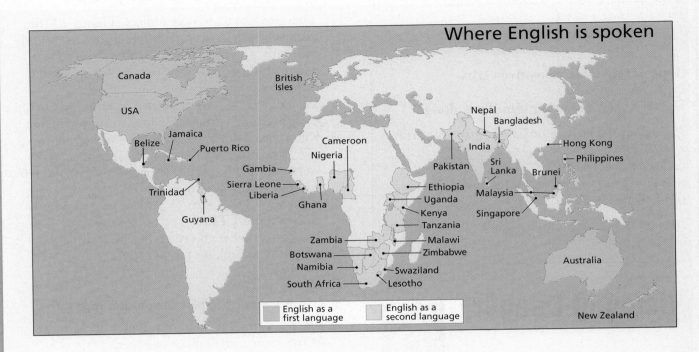

Where English is spoken

English as a first language
English as a second language

Towards a global language

How can Piotr in Poland talk to Françoise in France and make sure there are no misunderstandings? For a long time, people have felt the
5 need for a global language so that we can all talk to one another.

For a while it was thought that artificial languages would be the solution. Six hundred and fifty
10 languages have been tried and abandoned. The most successful artificial language has been Esperanto. Many people thought that it would become the global
15 language. It has not.

Instead, English has spread across the world and millions of people are learning it for a variety of reasons from listening to rock
20 music to understanding computers. Judging by present evidence, it is going to continue to spread:

- About eighty per cent of the data stored in the world's
25 computers is in English and you need it to surf the Internet.

- *Airspeak*, used by pilots and air-traffic controllers, and *policespeak* used in international
30 policing, are based on English.

- You need it for your holidays. Getting around in far-away corners of the globe is no problem if you speak English.

35 - You need it for entertainment. Four or five out of ten songs in the pop charts in most countries at any given time are sung in English.

40 - The World University, the first international university on a cable and satellite network, will broadcast in English.

English is by far the most widely
45 taught foreign language. In addition, some countries are introducing changes to their educational system: more children are to learn more English at an
50 earlier age. Of course many new learners are already familiar with the language: Hollywood and pop music have made sure of that.

English is not welcome
55 everywhere, however. Some nations consider the use of English to be a challenge to their national identity. Others simply want to stop the unwelcome invasion. The *Académie*
60 *Française*, an official body which protects and regulates the French language, has banned English words like *Walkman* in offical documents. It wants people to use
65 French words instead.

As a second language that allows easy communication across international borders, English is the answer to Piotr and Françoise's
70 problem. So it looks as if English will continue to be the language the world wants to speak.

Reading

Most writers have personal views – an angle – and will try to persuade readers to look at things in a certain way. It is important to recognise the writer's angle by asking yourself:
- What are the facts? What are the opinions?
- Does the author tell you whose opinions they are? (They might just be his/her own opinions.)
- Does the author give enough evidence for the facts presented?

2 Read the article again. Complete the table.

	Presented as fact or opinion?	If opinion whose is it?	If fact, do you think author gives enough evidence?
1 For a long time, people have felt the need for a global language.	F		Yes
2 Esperanto was going to become the world language.			
3 Most of the data stored in computers is in English.			
4 English is by far the most widely taught foreign language.			
5 In some countries, more children are going to learn more English at an earlier age.			
6 English is a challenge to a nation's identity.			
7 English will continue to be the language the world wants to speak.			

Grammar

Future and future in the past

1 Future
a) Predictions
English **will continue** to be the language the world wants to speak.
Judging by present evidence, it **is going to continue** to spread.
The writer thinks this will happen.

b) Arrangements
More children **are to learn** more English at an earlier age.
The authorities have arranged for this to happen in the future.

2 Future in the past

The past   Now
—————×————————×————————×—
thought   would be

People thought that artificial languages **would be/were going to be** the solution.
At the time, it was a prediction about the future.

3 Which of these sentences are predictions (P)? Which tell us about arrangements made by some authority, not the subject (A)?

EXAMPLE: 1 P

1 More children will learn English.
2 Soon pupils are to start learning English when they are seven.
3 In years to come, students are going to learn a second foreign language at university.
4 The students are to do grammar exercises every week.
5 They will also learn vocabulary.
6 Next year, all pupils are to get an English dictionary.
7 Students will work in pairs as well as on their own.

4 Rewrite the prediction sentences so that they indicate arrangements made by an authority.

EXAMPLE: 1 *More children are to learn English.*

5 Make sentences combining a phrase from **A** with the suitable phrase from **B**. Use *was/were going to* or *would*.

EXAMPLE: *Ricky and Tim thought they were going to/would have language problems during their round the world trip. They didn't, lots of people spoke English.*

A

1 Ricky and Tim/think/have language problems during round world trip
2 It/look as if/technology solve all problems
3 Competitors/believe/Walkman not popular
4 Doctors/think/Tim never walk
5 When I/get up/I/think/sunny all day
6 Miguel/think/learning English very difficult

B

> • create/more • not stop raining • lots of people/speak/English • he/know/a lot of words from English pop songs • Sony/sell/100 million • he/can run

Writing

6 Prepare to write a composition called 'A global language, do we need one?'

a) Match the columns.

The writer thinks . . .	He/she writes . . .
1 For example	a) It's important to remember that
2 As a conclusion, I want to say	b) This is not always the case
3 It's not (always) true	c) Take for instance
4 I think this is important	d) Bearing this in mind I think
5 Rembering what I've just said, I think	e) To sum up, I would say that

b) In groups, give your opinions and your reasons.
   1 Is a global language necessary?
   2 If it is, should the global language be English? Why (not)?
   3 How important is English in your country?
c) Report the group's views to the rest of the class.
d) Write your composition. Include both facts and opinions. You can use the information in the text on page 94 if you want to.

7 Which of these statements do you agree with?

1 BEATA: 'I have now finished *High Flyer*. I don't have to study English any more.'

2 COSTAS: 'I can now speak English. I can concentrate on French.'

3 NILGUN: 'I'm quite pleased with the English I've learnt. But I feel I've got to keep practising it so I don't forget it.'

Reading

8 Scan the text on page 97. Which of the comments in Exercise 7 does the writer agree with?

Listening

9 🔊 Read the text again. Then listen to four language learners talking about keeping up a foreign language. Which of the things in the text are mentioned?

Don't be a silly billy, keep up your English

Phew! Getting to the end of this book must have meant a lot of work for you. But you've done it! Bravo! Your English must be quite good now. However, there's still room for improvement. Besides, a language which is not practised soon gets rusty. Here are some things you can do to improve your English, or just make sure you don't forget it.

Formal learning

- Continue to study English at school or college.
5 - Join an English language school.
- Take private lessons.
- Aim to take one of the external examinations in English.
- Buy a video or audio cassette
10 English course, and follow it!

Informal learning which you can do on your own

15 - Listen to radio broadcasts or songs in English.
- Watch films or videos in English.
- Watch television programmes in English with cable or satellite television.
20 - Read in English. Anything! Books, newspapers, comics or magazines.
- Write down lists of words which are new to you. Check the meaning in the dictionary and try to learn them
25 – and use them.

Informal learning done with others

- Get a pen friend in an English
30 speaking country.
- Try to meet English speaking visitors to your town.
- Start exchange conversation sessions with a native speaker of English who lives near
35 you. You chat in English for half an hour and in your language for another half an hour.
- Start an English language club.

10 🖭 **Listen again. Which learner(s):**

1 asked for advice?
2 had already decided what to do?
3 decided what to do there and then?

Grammar

Intentions, decisions and asking for advice

What **shall/should** I do to keep up my English?
Can you give me some advice?

How will you keep up your English?
I know! I**'ll/will** get a pen friend.
I decided when I spoke.

I**'m going to read** in English every day.
I firmly intend to do it. I have already decided.

11 **Complete the sentences with** *will, shall* **or** *be going to.*

1 _____ I use a monolingual dictionary?
2 I _____ make sure I don't forget my English. I have registered for a course in Australia.
3 What shall I do? Oh yes, I know! I _____ join an English language club.
4 What sort of English books _____ I read?
5 _____ I add anything else to the list? I know! I _____ get a magazine too.
6 We _____ have conversation sessions with an Argentinian boy. That way, we won't forget our Spanish.
7 I've got it! I _____ read a newspaper in English once a week.

12 **What about you? What are you going to do about your English? Use the correct form to indicate those things you already intended to do and those you have just decided on (after reading the text).**

Revision

1 **Look at the photographs in the text.**

a) Can you name the people without reading the captions?

b) What was their occupation?

c) Make a list of things people in that occupation do. Compare your list with your partner's.

Reading

2 **Read these questions.**

1 What types of animal have been used for espionage?

2 How many methods of espionage are mentioned in the text? Name the newest and the oldest methods mentioned.

To find the answers, are you going to skim or scan the article? Why? Find the answers.

Twentieth-century spies

'My name is Bond . . . James Bond.' James Bond, agent 007, is perhaps the most famous spy in the world.

Mata Hari This Dutch dancer was employed by the French secret service. It is now said that she was in fact a very bad spy.

The tools of the trade

Invisible ink In the very early days, when spies wanted to send secret messages, they used invisible ink. The message was
5 written in lemon juice instead of ink. To read the message, the sheet of paper simply had to be warmed over a gentle flame, like that of a candle. The heat
10 cooked the lemon and the writing appeared: the message had reached its destination!

Radio The radio was a very useful tool for spies since it
15 allowed them to transmit up to eighty words per minute. In addition, because they were being made of lighter and lighter materials, radio sets were soon
20 able to be carried about easily and discreetly. The agents of the Special Operation Executive, an organisation whose aim was to help the resistance movements
25 in Europe to fight Hitler, used a radio weighing just 4 kilograms. With it agents could send messages to places 1000 kilometres away. The radio was
30 powered by a battery. To be recharged, the battery had to be connected to a bicycle: the power was produced by pedalling!

35 **Microfilm** The secret agent joined the workers at the gate of the weapons factory. Dressed like an ordinary worker he was able to walk in without being
40 spotted. Asked to fetch some plans from the factory files, he seized his chance: in just a few minutes, he managed to take photos of the designs for the
45 new weapons without any equipment being visible. How? He used a tiny camera hidden in his watch. From the 1950s, spies had a new ally: a camera which
50 could take microscopic photos. Because it was so small, the camera could be hidden in a watch, a pen or a small piece of jewellery. The information was
55 then read using a microscope. Microfilms were often cut into 'microdots'. One microdot measured half a millimetre and was capable of carrying a full
60 page of a document. Being so small microdots could be hidden under a postage stamp.

Computers Today, the computer is the most important
65 tool of espionage. Spies need to have a good knowledge of computer technology. This allows them to access computer networks illegally. By doing this,
70 they are able to obtain top secret information from banks, foreign governments and powerful corporations.

Unusual spies

75 • Simon the cat managed to cross the Yang Zijiang River to take a message to a Chinese general. Since 1950, the CIA (the American Central Intelligence
80 Agency) has been training different animals as spies. Secret services will soon be able to use dogs, seals and dolphins to spy on their enemies.

85 • It is believed that otters are the best animal agents: they can run, they can swim and they can penetrate enemy lines and then return with recorded
90 information.

3 Read the text again.

a) Fill in the first two columns of the chart.

Method of spying	How it worked	Extra information	(Dis)advantages
Coded messages	*e.g. numbers corresponding to line number and letter number in book. e.g. 2-2 = 2nd line, 2nd letter. Lists of numbers spelt words.*	*Popular. Used by the Russians until World War II.*	*Anyone could use it. Just needed a copy of the same book. But, so simple to use, had to change code often.*
Invisible ink		—	
Radio			
Microfilm			
Computer			

b) Using the notes in the first two columns of the chart, write a paragraph for the article about coded messages. Remember to use the Passive voice where necessary. Start like this:
The use of coded messages was a popular method of espionage. It was used by . . .

4 Prepare to write a report about the methods of spying in Exercise 3. Work in pairs.

a) Use the information in the article and your own ideas to make notes about the advantages and disadvantages of the methods.

b) Use your notes in a) to write a short report for a new network of spies. Recommend the best method(s)!
EXAMPLE: *Coded messages: On the positive side, this method could be used by anyone . . . . On the negative side, the code had to be changed often. Being so simple, this method was used by lots of spies and codes were easy to break.*

5 Could you be a top spy?

a) Who can decode this message first?
Clue: look at the text on page 98.

> 5-12, 10-5, 16-13, 17-16   23-20, 24-2
> 25-26, 28-9   35-10, 38-21, 40-6
> 41-15, 43-11, 47-4, 50-6, 54-5, 60-13
> 62-11, 64-6   26-18   67-4, 67-3

b) Send your partner a short coded message using the text on page 98.

Listening

6 Listen to parts of a radio programme about a famous French spy.

a) ▭ Each time the story stops, choose the alternative which describes what you think the narrator is going to say or talk about next.
1 how the police caught the criminal/the police didn't catch the criminal
2 other reasons *why* people spy/more about *how* spies spy for their country
3 why Cremet was so important/one of his adventures
4 the problem with the agent/the sort of things the new agent was able to do
5 Jean and Louise's life before 1927/after 1927

b) ▭ Listen to the complete programme and check your answers in a). Which words express the correct alternatives in a)?
EXAMPLE: *The bird had flown = the police didn't catch the criminal.*

7 ▭ Listen to the programme again and complete these sentences about Jean Cremet.

1 When the police went to the flat in Paris they thought *they would/were going to find Cremet there.*
2 When Cremet hired the new agent he didn't suspect . . .
3 Because Cremet had always admired Russia he probably thought that when he got there . . .
4 Cremet said goodbye to his daughter. He and his daughter couldn't predict then . . .
5 In 1927 it was impossible to predict that Cremet . . . in World War II.

The wider world

8 The *High Flyer* wider world quiz

You will need this board, two tokens and a dice.

a) To play the game, two teams take turns to roll the dice.
- Move your token the number of squares indicated.
- The other team will ask you a question on the category of your square. If you answer correctly, stay where you are. If you answer incorrectly, go back to the beginning!
- If you land on the same category more than once, you must answer a grammar question.
- The team to actually *land* on the last square and answer correctly is the winner.

b) Team A: Turn to page 104.
Team B: Turn to page 106.

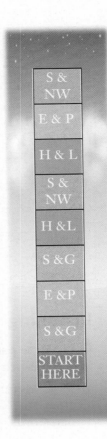

Project

9 **Make a board and more cards for the *High Flyer* wider world quiz.**

a) In groups, look through *High Flyer* and write new question cards for the game. You needn't write Grammar questions! Look at the question cards on pages 104 and 106 for ideas.

b) Make a larger board of your own to play the game with other people in your class.

Grammar practice

1 **Complete the sentences with *as, like,* or *as if/as though*. (Unit 20)**

1 Stop talking to me _____ you were my mother!
2 My brother worked _____ a baby sitter during the holidays.
3 Sit down and take a rest. You look _____ you need it.
4 Alice is a real chatterbox. She talks _____ a parrot.
5 Your English is very good. You speak almost _____ an English person!
6 In the James Bond films, Sean Connery was the first to star _____ James Bond.
7 I slept _____ a baby last night.

2 **Write comparisons using *as . . . as*. (Unit 20)**

EXAMPLE: 1 *You look as fresh as a lettuce.*
1 It's very hot but you look very fresh. Just like a lettuce!
2 The baby's skin is very soft. It reminds me of silk.
3 I must get a sun tan. My skin is very white. It looks like milk.
4 The boys' shirts were very white, like snow.
5 Her cheeks were round and red. They reminded me of an apple.

3 **Rewrite these sentences using present and past participle clauses. (Unit 21)**

EXAMPLE: 1 *I read the book before seeing the film.*
1 I read the book before I saw the film.
2 I saw the film with my brother, then I told my friends all about it.
3 Dracula must be one of the best horror films that has ever been made.
4 I ate an ice cream while I waited for my friend.
5 Mary's camera didn't break when she dropped it because it was made of very tough plastic.
6 The child hid under his bed because he was feeling scared.
7 My sister thinks the telephone is the best machine that was ever invented.
8 I bought a present for Dan and took it along to his birthday party.

4 **Complete these dialogues using *could, be able to* or *manage to*. (Unit 22)**

1 - It was a very difficult exam and I hadn't studied at all but somehow I _____ pass it.
 - You shouldn't do that. One day you won't be so lucky and you _____ to guess the answers.
2 - I'm sorry, Lucy. I _____ come to your party because we're going away for the weekend.
 - What a pity! You _____ meet my cousin John.
3 - Mozart _____ compose music at the age of four. What a genius!
 - Really? I _____ hardly speak at that age! Mind you I _____ kick a football pretty well. I bet Mozart _____ do that!
4 - When I got home I realised I didn't have a key so I _____ get in.
 - How did you _____ get in in the end?
 - I _____ climb in through the window but it was really hard!

5 Write these sentences out correctly. You need to put the verbs in the correct form and add articles when necessary. Make sure you put the particle of the phrasal verbs in the correct place. (Unit 22)

EXAMPLE: 1 *The teacher gets angry when the class laughs at other people's mistakes.*

1 teacher/get angry/when/class/laugh/at/other people's mistakes.
2 I/can/go/out/yesterday/because/I/be/ill.
3 Be/that/real story/or/you/make/up/it?
4 I/have to/turn/down/his invitation to party.
5 My parents/get/back/from work/until/after/I/go to/bed.
6 I/manage to/finish/my homework/and/teacher/tell/off/me.
7 Guess/who/I/run/into/at/shop?

6 Complete these sentences using *going to, will* or *is/are to*. (Unit 23)

1 I think in the end the hero ____ get the heroine in the soap opera. It's always like that!
2 Look at those huge clouds! It ____ rain. And we ____ get wet as usual.
3 There are new rules at school: from now on, we ____ start classes at 8 a.m. and finish at 3.30 p.m., we ____ wear a uniform for all school activities and everyone ____ do at least one hour's homework every evening! I'm sure students ____ like this at all.
4 There's no point in training so hard. We ____ lose the game again.
5 I don't agree with you. I think this time ____ win. The team is looking good.

7 Write sentences for these situations. (Unit 23)

a) Ask for advice.
 EXAMPLE: 1 *What shall/should I do to keep fit?*
 1 You're not very fit.
 2 You're not very good at Science. You want to improve your marks.
 3 You were rude to your mum. Now you want to find a way to say sorry.
b) You want to keep your weight down. What three things have you already decided to do?
 EXAMPLE: *I'm going to eat less chocolate.*
c) You're not very good at Science. What three things have you just decided to do to improve your marks?
 EXAMPLE: *I know! I'll talk less in class.*

Grammar

1 talk about scientific processes, developments and experiments using the passive voice in various forms. (Unit 19)
2 use a variety of fixed phrases which include a preposition. (Unit 20)
3 distinguish between *as . . .as, as, like* and *as if/though*. (Unit 20)
4 give additional information by using present and past participle clauses. (Unit 21)
5 describe actions we see and hear using *see/hear* + infinitive or *-ing*. (Unit 21)
6 talk about ability in the past and the future using *could, was/were able to, manage to* and *will be able to*. (Unit 22)
7 distinguish the different types of phrasal verb. (Unit 22)
8 make predictions about the future using *will* and *going to* and describe arrangements using *be to*. (Unit 23)
9 narrate events in the past which were destined to happen using *was going to* and *would*. (Unit 23)
10 ask for advice using *shall* and *should*. (Unit 23)
11 talk about intentions and decisions just made. (Unit 23)

Skills

READING

• identify the outlook of a newspaper. (Unit 20)
• read a text in the way that suits your purpose. (Unit 21)
• identify a writer's angle. (Unit 23)

WRITING

• write reports/accounts of scientific processes, developments and experiments. (Unit 19)
• write stories in a clear and interesting way. (Unit 21)

LISTENING

• reflect on what is being said and to predict what will follow as the speaker speaks. (Unit 19)

SPEAKING

• prepare and give informal talks. (Unit 19)
• take part in discussions intelligently. (Unit 20)
• keep a conversation going by using the correct intonation and expressions to encourage other speakers to continue. (Unit 22)

101

Unit 2 Exercise 14

Student A: You think David Clegg would be ideal for the job. Read these notes and list his advantages. Tell your partner what's on your list. Listen to your partner and make notes. Use all your information and the expressions in Exercise 14a on page 13 to persuade your partner that David is the better candidate.

Name: David Clegg
Age: 52
Nationality: American
Occupation: Doctor
Comments: Several previous expeditions. Has had minor health problems but passed training. Used to spending long periods of time alone.

Unit 7 Exercise 1

All of the information is true according to the study on Contemporary Juvenile Reading Habits.

Unit 8 Exercise 1

1 a
2 b (George the First was German.)
3 c
4 b

Unit 9 Exercise 1

Word missing from the title: *ecology*

Verdict

Your answer was correct: Congratulations! You are ecologically aware - or at least you know the vocabulary!

Your answer was incorrect: What's the matter, don't you know we must all learn to care for our planet?

Unit 22 Exercise 9

Student A: When you listen to your partner's description of his/her pictures, indicate that you are following and that you want him/her to continue. Use the expressions in the box and the information in Exercise 8 on page 92. Also let him/her know if you don't understand.

Unit 13 Exercise 12

Pair A: Read the listings that the other pair has written. Think of a few questions asking for clarification and explanation. You need to have enough information to be able to choose the best Pick of the day. Ask Pair B your questions. Answer Pair B's questions.

EXAMPLE: MARIA: *What kind of programme is* The Deep Blue?

ANA: *It's a factual programme about the sea.*

Post your listings on the classroom wall. Take a vote to choose the most exciting one.

Unit 14 Exercise 16

Student A: You think you have found a wonderful piece of treasure! Telephone your nearest museum and describe your find (picture 1). The person from the museum will tell you if you really have found some valuable treasure! Swap roles and listen to your partner describe his/her find. Look at pictures 2 and 3 and tell him/her what he/she has found.

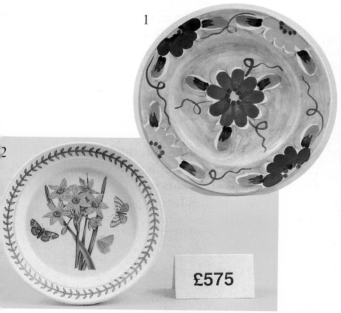

1

2

£575

3

30p

Unit 17 Exercise 11

Pair A: Read this dream. Tell Pair B about it in your own words. Then listen to Pair B's dream. Make notes about it. Turn back to page 73.

It is said that in 44 BC, Julius Caesar, the Roman leader, had a strange dream. He dreamt that he was flying in the sky above the clouds. There, he saw Jupiter, the most important Roman god. Julius Caesar flew to him and shook his hand.

At the same time Julius Caesar's wife, Calpurnia, dreamt that their house collapsed and that her husband was stabbed and died in her arms.

The next day, Julius Caesar was murdered. He was stabbed to death by Brutus, a Roman politician.

Unit 19 Exercise 8

WADDINGTONS
Rules for MONOPOLY
Registered Trade Mark
PROPERTY TRADING BOARD GAME
Players 2-6 Ages 8-Adult

Brief idea of the game

The idea of the game is to buy and rent or sell properties so that players increase their wealth: the wealthiest becomes the winner. Starting from 'GO', move the tokens around the board the number of spaces indicated by the dice. When a player's token lands on a space not already owned, (s)he may buy it from the Bank. The object of owning property is to collect rents from other players stopping there. If a player puts hotels or houses on the property, (s)he can charge much more rent. Community Chest and Chance cards give instructions that must be followed. The game is one of intelligent and amusing trading and excitement.

Unit 22 Exercise 9

Student B: When you listen to your partner's description of his/her pictures, indicate that you are following and that you want him/her to continue. Use the expressions in the box and the information in Exercise 8 on page 92. Also let him/her know if you don't understand.

Unit 24 Exercise 8

The *High Flyer* wider world quiz: Team A

a) Before you start the game, work out the answers to the grammar questions.
b) When it is your turn, ask Team B a question from your question card. The answers to the first four questions are given in *italics*.

S & NW	What do you call a person specialising in the study of plants? *A botanist*
E & P	What's the name of the pop group whose tour of Europe was called Zooropa? *U2*
S & G	What's the name of the white suit worn in karate? *A gi*
H & L	Having lost his wife, he marries Jane Eyre. Who is he? *Mr Rochester*
G	1 Complete this sentence with *as* or *like*. James Bond used his watch ____ a camera. 2 Say these two sentences in one using *as if/as though*. It was her first job as a secret agent. From her success you would think she had done that job all her life. 3 Rephrase this sentence using a passive construction. People say that there are spies in every country. 4 Say these two sentences in one. I saw a mysterious man. He took photos of the Embassy.

Key: S & NW = Science and the Natural World; E & P = Entertainment and People; S & G = Sports and Games; H & L = History and Literature; G = Grammar

Unit 10 Exercise 11

1 William Tell
2 Buffalo Bill
3 Pocahontas

Unit 2 Exercise 14

Student B: You think Georgina Shephard would be ideal for the job. Read these notes and list her advantages. Listen to your partner and make notes. Tell him/her your list of advantages. Use all your information and the expressions in Exercise 14a on page 13 to persuade your partner that Georgina is the better candidate.

> **Name:** Georgina Shephard
> **Age:** 28
> **Nationality:** British
> **Occupation:** Psychologist
> **Comments:** No previous experience. Very fit. Passed training course. Used to working with people as part of a team.

Unit 10 Exercise 10

Student A: Look at the pictures. They form half the story of Old Man Winter and Summer Queen. Describe them carefully to your partner and listen to his/her description of the missing pictures. Together, work out the correct order of the pictures.

Old Man Winter was in his snow kingdom.

'Please save him,' said Chief Glooksap.

Unit 13 Exercise 12

Pair B: Answer Pair A's questions. Then ask them to explain things about their programmes. You need to have enough information to be able to choose the best Pick of the day.

EXAMPLE: ANA: *What kind of programme is . . . ?*

Post your listings on the classroom wall. Take a vote to choose the most exciting one.

Unit 14 Exercise 16

Student B: You work for a museum. Someone telephones and says that they think they have found a wonderful piece of treasure. Listen to his/her description and look at pictures 1 and 2. Tell the caller if he/she really has found some valuable treasure! Swap roles and describe your find (picture 3).

Unit 17 Exercise 11

Pair B: Read this dream. Then listen to Pair A's dream. Make notes about it. Tell Pair A about your dream in your own words. Turn back to page 73.

Napoleon Bonaparte, first emperor of France, apparently had a disturbing dream one night in 1815. He dreamt that he was on the battlefield when suddenly, a black cat appeared and ran madly from one army to the other. The cat did this repeatedly. The battle ended in the defeat of the French army.

The next day, Napoleon and his army suffered a terrible defeat at the battle of Waterloo.

Unit 10 Exercise 10

Student B: Look at the pictures. They form half the story of Old Man Winter and Summer Queen. Describe them carefully to your partner and listen to his/her description of the missing pictures. Together, work out the correct order of the pictures.

Chief Glooksap went to see Summer Queen.

Unit 24 Exercise 8

The *High Flyer* wider world quiz: Team B

a) Before you start the game, work out the answers to the grammar questions.

b) When it is your turn, ask Team A a question from your question card. The answers to the first four questions are given in *italics*.

S & NW	What was the name of the project where students can have video conferences with classes around the world? *The Global Schoolhouse project*
E & P	What's the name of the explorer who crossed Antarctica on foot? *Sir Ranulph Fiennes*
S & G	How can anyone make - and lose! - a lot of money and have fun at the same time? *Playing Monopoly*
H & L	What's the name of the order of knights who became famous for fighting the wicked and helping the poor? *The Round Table*
G	1 Complete this sentence with *as* or *like*. Mata Hari was a dancer but she also worked _____ a spy. 2 Rephrase this sentence using *as if/as though*. Jean Cremet spoke Russian like a Russian but he was French. 3 Rephrase this sentence using a passive construction. People now believe that Mata Hari was a bad spy. 4 Say these two sentences in one. I heard a child. He was crying when I first heard him.

Key: S & NW = Science and the Natural World; E & P = Entertainment and People; S & G = Sports and Games; H & L = History and Literature; G = Grammar

Grammar reference

Ability

I Past

1 Ability in general: *could/was able to*
e.g. *Leonardo da Vinci **could/was able to** draw with one hand and write with the other at the same time.*
2 Ability on a specific occasion: *was able to* and *managed to*
e.g. *The Rosetta Stone contained an inscription in Egyptian hyeroglyphics and a translation in Greek. Scholars **managed to** or **were able to** work out what the hieroglyphics meant because they knew ancient Greek.*

Watch out! *Managed to* implies effort because something was difficult.

2 Future

will be able to and *will manage to*

Watch out! We also use *can* and *could* to talk about things we perceive through our senses.
e.g. *Can you hear what I hear?*

Adjective order

Opinion adjectives (*ugly, funny*) normally go before more factual adjectives (*woollen, Danish*).
e.g. *My grandfather was a funny plump French farmer.* ✓
e.g. *My grandfather was a ~~French plump~~ farmer.* ✗

Sometimes a comma is used to separate the adjectives in a list but not before *and*.

It is possible to use all the adjective types to describe one noun but it is in practice rare. We usually use other devices to write a full description.
e.g. *My grandmother was a lovely Brazilian woman. She was small and slim with grey hair.* rather than:
e.g. *My grandmother was a lovely small slim grey-haired Brazilian woman.*

Adjective + preposition

Further common adjective + preposition combinations:

by - amazed, impressed, surprised
e.g. *I was not **impressed by** the new boy's behaviour.*

of - aware, (in)capable, characteristic, full, scared
e.g. *The room was **full of** people.*

to - (un)accustomed, married, similar, related
e.g. *The Maths teacher is my uncle: he's **married to** my mum's sister.*

with - filled, compatible
e.g. *Is your computer **compatible with** mine?*

The best way to learn these combinations is to memorize them as set phrases.

Articles

I A/an

Apart from the uses on page 40, we also use *a/an*:
a) before we say what somebody or something is.
e.g. *Tom is **a** teacher.*
b) before an uncountable noun when it is qualified.
e.g. *We had **a very nice ham** for lunch.*

2 The

We also use *the*:
a) before musical instruments.
e.g. *John plays **the oboe** in the school orchestra.*
b) before an uncountable noun when it is followed by a qualifying phrase.
e.g. *I liked **the ham we had for lunch**.*
c) with superlative adjectives.
e.g. ***The tallest** people in the world are the Watusi men of Central Africa. They are often 2.3 metres tall.*
d) with the names of some geographical features.
- oceans and seas (***The** Atlantic, **The** Red Sea*)
- rivers (***The** Thames*)
- countries which include a countable noun (***The** United Kingdom*) or when they are plural (***The** Netherlands*)

Watch out! We do not use *the* before:
a) continents (*Asia*), lakes (*Lake Titicaca*).
b) uncountable nouns when referring to something in general. e.g. *I like pop music.*
c) possessives. e.g. *Have you seen **my** keys?*

As, as if/though, like

Clauses introduced by *as, as though, as if* or *like* are called clauses of manner.

I As and like are used:

a) to talk about the way someone behaves or the way something is done.
e.g. *Try to write your project **as** your teacher has shown you.*
Like + clause = more informal:
e.g. *There is no need to behave **like** you do in class.*
b) to compare ways of doing something.
e.g. *She tries to dress **like** a model.*
e.g. *My dad studied medicine **as** his father did before him.*
Watch out!
e.g. *Mary looks after Susan **like** a big sister. (Mary **isn't** her sister. It's a comparison.)*
e.g. ***As** the big sister, Mary has to set the example. (Mary **is** the big sister.)*

2 As if, as though

e.g. *At the party, Peter behaved **as if/as though** I didn't exist. He didn't even say hello! (But of course I **did** exist.)*
Watch out!
e.g. *Don't look at me as if I **were/was** crazy. (were = more formal)*
We often use *as if* and *as though* after verbs such as *feel, look, seem, sound* or *smell*.
e.g. *I **feel** as if I've **run** a hundred miles.*
e.g. *You **looked** as though you **had seen** a ghost.*

Be used to and get used to

1 When we want to talk about things or situations we find (un)familiar we use *(not) be used to* + noun phrase/verb-*ing*.
e.g. *Laika the dog, the first living creature in space, **wasn't used to life/living** in a spacecraft but she survived for several days until her oxygen ran out.*
2 When we want to talk about things or situations which are becoming less unfamiliar we use *get used to* + noun phrase/verb-*ing*.
e.g. *The experiment with Laika helped scientists realise that man could **get used to life/living** in a spacecraft for a certain period of time.*

Watch out!
e.g. *The astronaut **is used to living** in a spacecraft.* He has adapted to life there.
e.g. *Neil Armstrong, the first man on the moon, **used to work** for NASA.* He doesn't any more.

Clauses of concession

When we want to talk about two things, one of which contrasts with the other or makes it seem surprising, we use *even though* or *despite* to link them in one sentence.

I *even though* + sentence
e.g. *My mother loves Italian operas **even though** she can't understand the words.*
We can reverse the order of the clauses. In this case we use a comma to separate them.
e.g. ***Even though** she can't understand the words, my mother loves Italian operas.*
We can use *although* or *though* in the same way as *even though*.

2 *despite* +   noun
                    verb-*ing*
                    the fact that + sentence
e.g. *Mozart composed about 1,000 pieces of music **despite the fact that** he died young.*
As with *even though*, we can reverse the order of the clauses. We can use *in spite of* in the same way as *despite*.

Conditional clauses

I First conditional: *If* + Present Simple + *will or may or can* + infinitive
e.g. *If you **visit** China you **can** see the Great Wall.*

2 Second conditional: *If* + Past Simple + *would or might or could* + infinitive
e.g. *If you **had** fifteen books on a shelf and you **arranged** them in every possible combination, and if you **made** one change every minute, it **would** take 2,487,996 years to make them all.*

3 Third conditional: *If* + Past Perfect + *would or might or could* + *have* + Past Participle
e.g. *If Columbus **hadn't used** the wind, he **might** never **have reached** America.*

Variation: *If* + Past Perfect + *would* + infinitive
e.g. *My grandmother says that **if** she **had eaten** as many sweets as I do, she **wouldn't** still **have** all her teeth now.* The condition refers to the past but its consequence refers to the present. We are imagining how the consequence would be different now in different past circumstances.

Watch out! These words can replace *if* in conditional clauses:
Unless (= *if . . . not*)
e.g. *My dentist says I'll lose my teeth **unless** I cut down on the amount of sweets I eat.*
Provided/providing (that), so long as, as long as (= *if, but only if*) Used when one thing is necessary in order for another to happen.
e.g. *We can leave school at lunch time **as long as** our parents give their permission.*

It's time

We use *it's time* + subject + past tense to criticise or complain or when we think someone should have done something earlier.
e.g. *What a silly joke. **It's time** you **grew up**!*

Watch out!
1 To make the criticism stronger we can say *It's about/high time . . .*
2 To make the criticism less strong we can use a negative question. e.g. ***Isn't it time** Rick got a job?*

Needn't, need to, needs doing

I Talking about things which are necessary or very important
a) ***Need to*** can replace *must* or *have to* when we know the subject.
Past: *needed to*
e.g. *Greek sailors in the fifth century **needed to** know the weather conditions at sea.*
b) ***Needs doing*** means *needs to be done*. We use it when we don't know the agent or the agent isn't important.
Past: *needed doing*

2 Absence of obligation
needn't = not considered necessary by the speaker. It can refer to the present and to the future.
don't need to/don't have to = not considered necessary by someone in authority. It refers to the present.

Watch out!
e.g. *I **didn't need to** go so early.* = It wasn't necessary to go so early and I knew that at the time. (Therefore I didn't go early.)
e.g. *You **needn't have** come so early.* = It wasn't necessary to come so early but you didn't know that at the time so you went early.

Participle clauses

1 Present Participle: infinitive + *-ing*
This replaces active constructions.
a) Time
e.g. ***Since seeing*** *the film, I have been having rather strange dreams.* (= **Since I saw** *the film . . .*)
b) Reason
e.g. ***Possessing*** *extraordinary powers, a girl in France could knock over heavy pieces of furniture with a gentle touch.* (= **Because she had** *these powers she could . . .*)
c) Relative clauses
e.g. *People* **coming** *into contact with the 'electrical girl' got electric shocks.* (= *People* **who came** *into contact . . .*)

2 Past Participle: infinitive + *-ed*
This replaces passive constructions.
a) Reason
e.g. ***Convinced*** *that the area was not safe, he didn't leave his hotel for two weeks.* (= **Because** *he* **was convinced** *. . .*)
b) Relative clauses
e.g. *The message system used in our school is very good.* (= *The message system* **which is used** *. . .*)

3 Perfect participle: *having + Past Participle*
This is used to make it clear that one action was complete before a second one started.
e.g. ***Having flown*** *into a belt of cold air, a large flock of ducks froze to death.*
First action: The ducks flew into a belt of cold air.
Second action: The ducks froze to death.

Passive voice

Form: *to be* + Past Participle of another verb (+ *by* + agent)
Tense: carried by the auxiliary *be*
Examples:
Present Continuous: *is/are being* + Past Participle
Past Continuous: *was/were being* + Past Participle
Modal verbs: *can/will/could be* + Past Participle

Further uses
1 When people in general are the agents and you are reporting what they think, say or believe. In this case we use the impersonal pronoun *it*.
e.g. **It is said that** *the house on the hill is haunted.*
2 When you don't want to say who did the action or you want to distance yourself from your actions.
e.g. MOTHER TO CHILD: *If you don't get good marks, you* ***will be grounded***.

Phrasal verbs

1 Intransitive verbs
Intransitive verbs don't take an object.
You cannot separate the particle from the verb.

Watch out! Some verbs can be used with or without an object. In other words, they can be both transitive and intransitive but their meaning is usually different:
get back (I) - to return (usually) home
e.g. *When I got back, mum and dad were waiting for me.*

get back (T) - to be given something that you used to have e.g. *We got our projects back last week.*
Also: break down, dress up, fill in, get in, give in, keep up, turn away, turn up. Look these verbs up in your dictionary. Most dictionaries will indicate whether a phrasal verb is transitive (T) or intransitive (I) and they will usually give an example sentence.

2 Transitive verbs
These verbs have an object and you can separate the verb from its particle.
e.g. *He* ***made up*** *the story./He* ***made*** *the story* ***up***.

Remember
I don't believe your story. You are ***making*** *it* ***up***.
You are ***making up*** *that story about ghosts in the school.*
Also: bring up, call off, cross out, dream up, get out of, hand out, let down, put away, put forward, win over. Look these verbs up in your dictionary.

Watch out!
1 Some transitive phrasal verbs are not separable even if the object is a pronoun:
e.g. *He* ***cares about*** *other people. He* ***cares about*** *them.*
Also: believe in, come across, depend on, do without, get over, go into, look at, look through, refer to, wait on. Look these verbs up in your dictionary.
2 A small group of transitive verbs are always separated from their particle by the object:
e.g. *Annie* ***asked*** *Tom/him* ***out***. (= invited him to go out with her)
Also: invite someone out, invite someone over, order someone about, tell two things/people apart. Look these verbs up in your dictionary.

Remember
The best way to learn phrasal verbs is to memorize them and use them!

Possession

Remember
When we want to indicate possession we can use:

1 possessive determiners e.g. *my, your, our, her.*
Watch out!
a) *it's* = *it is*. The possessive determiner is *its*.
b) When you talk about a specific part of somebody's body you usually use a possessive determiner.
e.g. *What's she got in* ***her*** *hand?*
But if you describe an action someone does to a part of your or someone else's body, you use *the*.
e.g. *The ball hit me on* ***the*** *head.*
c) When you want to talk about an action you do to yourself or other people do to themselves you use a possessive determiner.
e.g. *You should clean* ***your*** *teeth after every meal.*

2 Apostrophe s ('s)
Watch out!
a) The apostrophe *s*, like possessive determiners, is most often used with living things.
e.g. *A **zebra's** stripes are as individual as human fingerprints.*
b) You can use apostrophe *s* after nouns and names referring to places in order to specify something in that place. e.g. **London's** biggest airport
c) You can use apostrophe *s* for time references.
e.g. *He has done a good **day's** work.*

3 the . . . of
This is used with objects. e.g. *The lead **of** an average **pencil** will draw a line 56 km long.*

Preference

1 Prefer
e.g. *Susan **prefers** Oasis **to** Blur.*
e.g. *I would **prefer** (not) to talk about it.*

2 Would rather
a) preference involving one person
e.g. *I would **rather** listen to Blur **than** to Oasis.*
e.g. *My mother would **rather** not listen to any music now.*
b) preference involving more than one person
e.g. *I would **rather you** didn't come to see me any more.*

Purpose

1 Same subject for both clauses
to, *in order to* and *so as to*

Watch out!
a) In the affirmative *to*, *in order to* and *so as to* are inter-changeable.
e.g. *A man changed his name to Zeke Zzzypt **to/in order to/ so as to** be the last name in the local telephone directory.*
b) In the negative, you can use only *in order to* and *so as to*.
e.g. *Abe Abbey would like to change his name ~~not to~~/**in order not to/so as not to** be the first name on his teachers' lists.*
c) You can reverse the order of the clauses. In this case use a comma to separate them:
e.g. ***In order to** be the last name in the local telephone directory, a man changed his name to Zeke Zzzypt.*

2 Same or different subject for each clause
so (that) and *in order that*
This type of purpose clause usually includes a modal verb.

Watch out!

Main clause	Purpose clause
Present tense or Present Perfect	*can*, *may*, or *will*

e.g. *Australian Aborigines who are widowers **wear** a lump of mud in their beard **so that** people **can** see they are looking for a new wife.*

Main clause	Purpose clause
Past tense	*could*, *might*, *should* or *would*

Recommendation

Had better
had better = should/ought to
Watch out!
1 Used with *I* or *we* it indicates an intention.
e.g. *We **had better** walk back now. It's getting dark.*
2 Used with *you*, it indicates a warning or advice.
e.g. *You**'d better** not forget to do your homework again.*
3 If you want to make your advice sound more polite, you can use a negative question.
e.g. ***Hadn't** you **better** go now?*

Relative clauses

1 Defining relative clauses with prepositions
a) In informal situations we put the preposition towards the end of the clause and often omit the relative pronoun.
e.g. *You are the only **girl** (**who/that**) I care **about**. Will you marry me?*
e.g. *This is the **moment** (**which/that**) I've been waiting **for**.*
b) In formal English the preposition goes before the relative pronoun.
e.g. *She was the only girl **about whom** he cared.*
e.g. *This was the moment **for which** he had been waiting.*

Watch out! e.g. *She was the only girl ~~about that/who~~ he cared.* ✗

2 Non-defining relative clauses.
Non-defining relative clauses cannot be used without a relative pronoun.
e.g. *Mini skirts, **which** are fashionable now, were first worn in the 1960s.*
It is not possible to use *that* instead of *who* or *which* in non-defining relative clauses.
e.g. *Mary Quant, **who** is an English designer, invented the mini skirt.*

Watch out! Non-defining relative clauses are used to give additional but not essential information. If we omit the non-defining clause, we are still left with a complete idea.
e.g. *Mary Quant, ~~who is an English designer,~~ invented the mini skirt.*
—> *Mary Quant invented the mini skirt.*

Reported speech

1 Indirect questions.
Sometimes we use an indirect question form for politeness.
e.g. ***Do** you sell party hats?* —> ***Can/could** you tell me if you sell party hats?*
e.g. ***How much** do they cost?* —> ***Can/could** you tell me **how much** they cost?*
Note that the question marks used here refer to the *Can/could* part of the indirect question.

2 Reporting advice

a) Suggesting what someone else should do.

e.g. TEACHER TO SARAH: *'Why don't you take special classes?'*

—-> *The teacher* **suggested that** *Sarah* **should** *take special classes.*

Also: *recommend/advise that . . . should*

e.g. TEACHER TO STUDENTS: *'You should study all the time, not only for exams.'*

—-> *The teacher* **recommended/advised/urged** *students* **to** *study all the time . . .*

Watch out! e.g. *Teachers* ~~suggested~~ *students* ~~to~~ *study all the time.* ✗

b) Giving general advice, not mentioning the person we are advising.

e.g. FRIEND: *'Let's have a party.'*

—-> *My friend* **suggested having** *a party.*

Also: *recommend/advise + -ing*

So/such

When *so* comes before an adjective/adverb it makes the meaning of the adjective/adverb stronger.

(That) + sentence following *so* + adjective/adverb introduces the result of that stronger adjective/adverb.

e.g. *On 4 September 1981 a tornado hit Ancona in Italy. It was* **so strong (that)** *it lifted a baby asleep in his pram 15 m into the air and set the pram down safely 100 m away. The baby was sleeping* **so soundly (that)** *it didn't wake up during this time!*

such + that is used to produce the same meaning.

Remember

such a/an + adjective + singular noun

such + adjective + plural/uncountable noun

e.g. *The winds at the centre of a tornado can reach* **such an incredible speed** *(644 kph)* **(that)** *they can lift whole houses.*

Watch out! You can use *so* + *many/few/much/little* and *such a lot of* in the same way.

e.g. *An average galaxy has* **such a lot of/so many** *stars* **(that)** *to count them all would take 1000 years at the rate of three a second.*

Stative verbs

These are verbs which are not normally used in the continuous form. The continuous form is normally used with deliberate actions, those you decide to do. Examples of stative verbs are *see, hear* and *smell* because if your eyes are open and there is nothing wrong with your ears or your nose, you see, hear and smell things even if you don't want to.

e.g. *What do you* **see** *when you stand at the window?*

Watch out! A number of verbs may or may not be used in the continuous form, depending on their meaning.

e.g. *smell something: The dog* **is smelling** *my lunchbox. It must be hungry!*

smell of something: I love your perfume. It **smells of** *roses.*

e.g. *be* (behave): *Why* **are you being** *so nice all of a sudden?*
be (+ quality): *He* **is** *very nice.*

e.g. *hear* (receive news or letters): *You* **will be hearing** *from us again.*

e.g. *feel* + emotion or physical condition: *Lisa went home because she* **wasn't feeling** *well.*

But: *This water* **feels** *hot.*

Tenses

I The Past

a) The **Past Simple** is used to talk about:

- situations which existed over a period of time in the past.

e.g. *We* **had** *a friendly teacher but he* **told** *pretty bad jokes.*

- events that happened at a particular time in the past.

e.g. *I* **read** *a book yesterday but it* **wasn't** *very good.*

b) The **Past Continuous** is used to:

- contrast a situation with an action which started after the situation had begun.

e.g. *'Sorry I'm late, sir. When the alarm went off I* **was dreaming** *about football,' said Bobby to his teacher. 'And they played extra time!'*

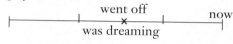

Also: *Bobby* **was always making up** *excuses for being late.* For frequently repeated actions in the past. This annoys the speaker.

c) The **Present Perfect** is used to talk about:

- something which happened in the past but you don't mention exactly when.

e.g. *I* **have heard** *his bad news.*

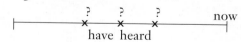

- something that started in the past, continues to the present and will probably continue for some time into the future.

e.g. *The students in this class* **have learnt** *a lot of English.*

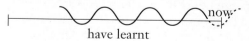

Remember

With this tense you can't use time expressions which place the action at a definite time in the past.

e.g. *I* ~~have heard~~ *a good joke* ~~yesterday~~. ✗

d) The **Present Perfect Continuous** is used to emphasise the duration of an action or event which continues up to the present and into the future or which has just finished.

e.g. *I've **been working** here for two months.*

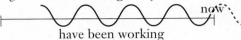

e) The **Past Perfect** is used to talk about events or situations which happened or began before a particular time in the past.

e.g. *When I got there I realised I **had left** my wallet behind.*

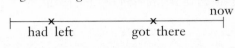

f) The **Past Perfect Continuous** is used to emphasise:
- the duration of a continuous action occurring before a particular point in the past.

e.g. *The man **had been waiting** for a long time before they brought his food.*

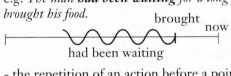

- the repetition of an action before a point in the past.
e.g. *Georgina **had been calling** Mark all morning. She finally managed to speak to him that afternoon.*

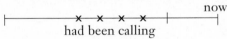

2 The Future

a) Predictions: *will* + infinitive and *be going to*
e.g. *(Experts think that) next year there **is going to/will** be an earthquake.*

Watch out!
- *Will* is also used to talk about decisions you have just made. e.g. *This club sounds like fun. **I'll join** tomorrow.*
- *Going to* is also used to talk about firm intentions. The speaker has already decided to do something.
e.g. *Next year, **I'm going to** learn Japanese. I've already registered for the course.*

b) Official arrangements for the future: *be + to + infinitive*
e.g. *Starting next year all students at this school **are to learn** two foreign languages.*

c) Personal arrangements for the future (Present Continuous) and **programmed actions** (Present Simple)
e.g. *I'm spending the summer in New Zealand. My plane leaves on Wednesday night.*

Watch out! You normally have to use a time expression with these tenses to avoid confusion.

d) Talking about **future events in the past:** *was/were going to* and *would*
e.g. *Peter **was going to** be in a play but he got ill so he couldn't.*

Watch out! These constructions usually imply that what we had expected to happen didn't happen.

Too, enough, not enough

Too = excess; enough = sufficiency; not enough = insufficiency

Watch out!
1 *Too* and *very* do not mean the same.
~~I'm too happy to meet you.~~ ✗
*I'm **very** happy to meet you.* ✓
2 You can use *too* before *many*, *much* and *few*.
e.g. *If you have eaten **too much** garlic, chew some fresh parlsey: it will take away the smell.*
3 *Enough* always comes after an adjective.
4 e.g. ***You** are too young/(not old enough) **to watch** the film.*
The film is for older people. **You cannot watch** it.
But also:
e.g. ***The chicken** was too hot/(not cool enough) **to eat**.* The chicken was very hot. **We couldn't eat** it.
5 *Enough* always comes before a noun.
e.g. *The human body contains **enough fat** to make seven bars of soap.*

Wish

1 *Wish (that)/if only* + Past Simple
This expresses regret about a present situation.
Watch out!
a) We can put *wish* in the past and leave the second verb in the Past Simple too.
b) *I wish I/he/she/it **was/were**. Was* is more common in conversation.
c) *Wish* + Past Simple: Past Simple doesn't change in reported speech.

2 *Wish (that)/if only* + Past Perfect
This expresses regret about a past situation.
Wish can be changed to *wished* as above.

3 *Wish (that)/if only* + would + infinitive
This expresses regret or a complaint about someone else's behaviour. We think he/she should change his/her behaviour and we know he/she can do it if he/she wants to.
e.g. *Three men were stuck on a desert island when a genie came out of a bottle and offered them one wish each.*
  'If only I hadn't taken the boat (2)! I wish I was back with my family and friends (1),' said the first man and he disappeared back home.
  'I miss my family too. I wish I was with them (1),' said the next man and he too disappeared.
  'It's very lonely here now, genie. I wish you would bring my friends back to keep me company(3)!' said the third man who wasn't very bright.

Watch out! *Wish* and *would* cannot have the same subject.
e.g. ~~I wish I would have more fun.~~ ✗